ISBN: 9781290184991

Published by:
HardPress Publishing
8345 NW 66TH ST #2561
MIAMI FL 33166-2626

Email: info@hardpress.net
Web: http://www.hardpress.net

CHARLES KINGSLEY

CHARLES KINGSLEY

CHRISTIAN SOCIALIST AND SOCIAL REFORMER

BY THE

REV. M. KAUFMANN, M.A.

AUTHOR OF
"CHRISTIAN SOCIALISM;" "SOCIALISM: ITS NATURE, ITS DANGERS,
AND ITS REMEDIES;" "UTOPIAS; OR, SCHEMES OF SOCIAL IMPROVEMENT FROM
SIR THOMAS MORE TO KARL MARX;" "SOCIALISM AND COMMUNISM IN
THEIR PRACTICAL APPLICATION," ETC., ETC.

Methuen & Co.

18, BURY STREET, LONDON, W.C.

1892

RICHARD CLAY & SONS, LIMITED,
LONDON & BUNGAY.

Dedicated

TO CONSTANCE, MARCHIONESS OF LOTHIAN,

Whose conscientious endeavours to minister to the necessities and to ameliorate the condition of the people in town and country, and experience in so doing, is a proof in point that what Charles Kingsley held up as ideal in fiction is translatable into fact;

That the progress of democracy does not by any means preclude a happy relationship of mutual affection and esteem between the lady of the manor and her dependents;

That the "silver link of sympathy" may yet unite the hearts of those born in high station and in low;

That is, where nobility of mind and heart becomes the parent of courteous kindliness in the one, and courteous recognition in the other;

And that where aristocracy of birth is accompanied by that of merit, so far from discouraging popular aspirations, it will help rather than hinder social progress in what is best in all classes.

PREFACE.

THIS Preface, like the dog Cerberus, has three heads, but only briefly to guard against three misconceptions at the entrance of this volume. 1. It is a monograph, not a biography, of Charles Kingsley, its object being simply to present one aspect of his life, as a social and sanitary reformer, and this in the setting and framework of the thought, feelings, and condition of his time, with the light of our own thrown upon the picture to present a distinct view of his social aims, and to show how far what he aspired after has been attained, and what remains of achievements yet to be accomplished in the future. 2. As it is a tolerably well-known fact that the late Mrs. Kingsley strongly objected to any biography of her husband, it should be mentioned that the present work was undertaken before her death, and with the full knowledge and cordial consent of the family. 3. Nothing contained in this volume has appeared in print before. Two independent articles in reviews, afterwards incorporated in the author's work on Christian Socialism, were published, indeed, as fragments of the subject before the reader here, but except for the fact that they are founded on the same materials, they are not otherwise connected with it. To these prefatory remarks may be added the hope that this condensed view of Kingsley's words and works on social subjects may help in stimulating and directing enthusiasms and efforts in our own generation among that numerous class of readers who take an interest in social questions.

May, 1892.

CONTENTS.

CHARLES KINGSLEY.

INTRODUCTION.

To understand the man and his social mission we must have before our mind a clear picture of the times in which he lived, and the condition of the people which called forth his generous sympathy and chivalric efforts in the cause of social reform. Of this, therefore, we will give a brief sketch before entering upon the main subject. The year 1848 marks an important epoch in the history of labour; it threatened to prove a critical year in the history of modern European society. The signal of a great rising had been given by the outbreak of the Revolution in Paris. The significance of that event was the self-assertion of the Proletariat, as such, dictating to the State what should be done on its behalf. It was the starting-point of a movement which has increased in force and momentum ever since; Social Democracy had become a self-conscious force.

State socialism was accepted as a principle in the

B

French Chamber by the establishment of national workshops, and thus gave a powerful impulse to the creation
of co-operative associations outside it. The Revolution
itself was a social revolution, the result of social distress
producing discontent among the masses; it amounted
to a declaration of war between the lower and the
middle classes. Since 1830 a differentiation had been
going on between capital and labour. The friction
became more and more irksome as it became more and
more evident that the power of capital had immensely
increased with the use of machinery, whilst the de-
pendence of labour on the rich capitalists was rendered
more galling since the vast increase of wealth did not
raise the toilers into a better position. Plutocracy had
become the new tyrant, and factory labour its slave.
In this new industrial society the gulf between rich
and poor was becoming wider every day. The Bourgeoisie
had displaced the privileged orders in the seat of power,
money had become the master of the situation, but the
era of steam and speculation, so far from promoting the
interest of the manual labourer, had tended to lower
wages, and to increase the prices of the necessaries of
life and other commodities in the enlarged demand
for greater self-indulgence among all classes. Labour
was chained to the triumphal chariot of "industrial
progress." It was the era of "free labour," but the
labourers who had helped to procure liberty, fighting
on the side of the middle class against the aristocracy,
now had learned that the cry of liberty was an empty
phrase, that in the very fact of free contract lay the

secret of greater inequality. They were angry beyond measure with the industrial despots, who dictated terms which it was impossible to refuse. True they were at liberty to refuse to labour at the terms offered. But in that case their families would starve. Capital had become omnipotent, the labourer was at its mercy, when at last, driven to despair by distress and famine, the populace revolted, and from Paris the spirit of revolt spread to Berlin and Vienna, and even to London. In Prussia and Austria the tricolour was unfurled as the emblem of German unity, and the symbol of Liberty, Equality, and Fraternity. In England the "People's Charter" was the formula which captivated the imagination of the populace. People had not learned even yet how to dissociate the social from the political elements of revolution, though the dim notion prevailed that in the Legislature, if anywhere, the battle must be fought between the men and their new masters. Thus it happened that in the same eventful month of March, in 1848, when barricades were raised by workmen and students in Vienna, and the King of Prussia was compelled at the dictation of the mob to do honour bare-headed to the remains of those who had fallen fighting behind the barricades of Berlin, the Duke of Wellington made preparations on a large scale in view of the great Chartist demonstration on the 10th of April in London, and the troops were kept in readiness for possible eventualities. The bridges were barricaded, the bank and state offices and public buildings were carefully provisioned—everything in short was done to prevent a repetition on a larger scale of those riots in London, Glasgow, Edinburgh, Liverpool, and other large towns during the month of March. London was in a state of panic. The demands of the Proletariat were much the same all over Western Europe. Thus, in Germany one of the clauses of the programme submitted to the Frankfort Parliament contained suggestions for a settlement of the differences between labour and capital by a "special ministry of labour," which "should check usury, protect workmen, and secure them a share in the profits of work."

In this country the Charter was to bring about pretty much the same effects by means of a larger and more direct representation in Parliament of the people's interests. There was nothing revolutionary in these demands, but the animus which inspired them, and the popular commotion aroused by the agitation, spread terror among the well-to-do classes.

On the Continent the "rule of Bureau and Bayonet" had added intensity to the virulence of social discontents. Here, too, popular complaints had not been wanting ever since 1832, when, after the agitation of the Reform Bill, it was said that instead of promoting the interests of the people it had practically disenfranchised labour, and rendered the moneyed class more powerful than it had been before the passing of that Bill. There were loud complaints, too, raised against the working of the new Poor Law, but the chief causes of discontent were in the first instance the "horrors of the factory system," and the temporary effects of the intro-

duction of steam in displacing manual labour, intensified
later on by over-production, with stagnation in trade
and the reduction of wages for its consequences. It
led to many acts of violence, such as smashing of
machinery, and setting fire to mills, and burning of
hay-ricks in country districts. Scarcity of work, low
wages, food at high prices, long-protracted hours of
labour, even in mining districts, including female and
child labour (in spite of legislation for their protection
since 1833, mainly through the exertion of Lord
Shaftesbury), failure of the crops, commercial reaction
after excessive speculation—all these produced misery
and privation, suffering and distress, which eventually
brought in their train serious disturbances encouraged
or organized by Chartist agitators. Military force had
to be called in to quell insurrection in the coal districts,
in the Potteries, and in Manchester. Other manu-
facturing towns in the north were kept in terror by
bands of excited workmen off and on since 1842.
The potato famine in Ireland in 1846 glutted the labour
market in England, and produced a further depression
of wages. Things went on from bad to worse in 1848.
The time had come, so it seemed to many, which Lord
Ashley had foretold in one of his speeches in Parliament
in 1843, when he had said—

"The danger is wider, deeper, fiercer, and no one who
has heard these statements, and believes them, can hope
that twenty years more will pass without some convulsion,
some displacement of the whole system of society,"—

a saying which the author of *Perils of the Nation*, which

appeared in the same year, fully endorsed, adding that, "if some stop be not put to the existing mischief (the growth of capital, with the growth *pari passu* of misery and distress), *a few years more must land us in a bloody revolution!*" Nor was it hard for the social agitators to convince excited mobs that "the panacea for all grievances is to be found in revolution." In short there was a general alarm.

Socialism and Chartism were rampant, and to meet the danger of the hour, F. D. Maurice and his followers, guided by his genius and moderated by his wisdom, struck out a new line so as to bring the Church home to the people's heart and to plead the people's cause before their masters, taking their stand on the broad platform of ecclesiastical and social reform. What they pleaded for was a resolute return to the principles of Christianity freed from later accretions of ossified officialism and dogmatic harshness, and the repellent self-assertion of class pride among the clergy and religious laity. In their opinion it had become necessary to remind the religious world that modern society rests on a Christian basis; that, accordingly, all social arrangements must be brought to the test of New Testament morality, that the organization of labour by means of association or co-operation implies the cultivation of those Christian virtues of mutual trust and forbearance, readiness for self-sacrifice and subordination, without which these social bonds would prove ineffectual. They affirmed, and among them more distinctly and emphatically than the rest, Charles Kingsley, that selfishness and the quest of self-interest is the main cause of our present social difficulties, for is it not the selfish pursuit of each individual and class without regard to the claims of society as a whole which lies at the root of social antagonism and social war? The war of free competition being accepted as a law of nature and lauded as the prime motive force of industrial progress, and the principle "every one for himself" being consecrated into a moral precept which, if obeyed by each individual or section of society representing a given class interest, would promote the happiness of all according to the pre-established laws of economic harmony, what follows from such principles but an internecine warfare of one against all, ending in the loosening and ultimate destruction of all social bonds? Hence the importance of a unifying force and a process of re-union by Christianity as a principle, and the Christian Church embodying it. "If the priests of the Lord are wanting to the cause now, woe to us!" cries Kingsley in a letter to Ludlow in 1850. The words confirm the earnest anxiety and apprehension which filled the hearts of the Christian socialists, and made them stand out from among the body of the clergy and religious laity as God-sent apostles of a new social era.

Maurice speaks of Kingsley as the "Thalaba with a commission to slay magicians and put the Eblis band which possesses our land to rout. I am jealous of anything which is likely to turn him out of his predestined course and may make him waste the God-given strength." It will be the object of this book to show how far Charles Kingsley corresponds to this description, and to what extent he succeeded in verifying this glowing prediction of his revered friend and master.

CHAPTER I.

EARLY LIFE, EDUCATION, AND SURROUNDINGS; PREPARATION FOR THE WORK.

ALTHOUGH this does not pretend to be a biography, but simply an attempt to present one aspect of a life's history, it is none the less interesting and important to notice how far descent, inherited traits of character, the circumstances of early life and training, and the current of events were instrumental in preparing the subject of this sketch for his public career. Charles Kingsley had no reason to be ashamed of his ancestors. He was born in 1819, "under the brow of Dartmoor," and inhaled, so to speak, the spirit of daring of the men of Devon which he so graphically describes in his most popular story, *Westward Ho!* From his mother, who, though of English parentage, was born in the West Indies, he inherited the love of luxuriant scenery and romantic sentiment, and that tendency to aristocratic condescension, in spite of his popular sympathies, which Europeans acquire who live in the East or the Tropics, a tone of mind which made him in his popular leanings a democratic Tory rather than a follower of what is now called Tory Democracy. His father was a man of good points, a country gentleman by birth and habits, a clergyman by force of circumstances, but none the less faithful in the discharge of his duties, a lover of art, a sportsman, a natural historian. From him the son probably inherited that "healthy materialism" which somewhere he commends, and his bent towards "muscular Christianity," a phrase associated with his name which he never liked. He has been called a "bold thinker and a bold rider," both in consequence of a healthy physique and the possession of a healthy mind in a healthy body bequeathed to him by both parents. The more subtle and poetic appreciation of the mysterious charm of nature and the power of artistic presentment were probably owing to the combined influence of both parents, aided by surrounding conditions. His early childhood was spent in the great Fen country. The effect on his mind of its flat scenery and the wide sweep of the horizon of the Lincolnshire meres, hidden in mist, or suffused with the after-glow of the setting sun, were never forgotten, and in the prelude to *Hereward the Wake*, a hero in whom, if we mistake not, the author sometimes portrays himself, though perhaps unconsciously, we are given to understand how the sturdy manliness of the Lowlander is generated by the sense of freedom as his eye wanders unimpeded over a vast expanse of open country. Here, in the absence of the overpowering sense of natural forces which inspire man with fear in the hill country, is generated a spirit of independence. These physical accidents, as

Kingsley frequently remarks, exercise an important influence on spiritual development. The antiquity of the house in which he was born, Barnack Rectory, built in the fourteenth century, with its haunted chamber, helped, no doubt, to call out the spirit of chivalry which lends a special charm to his character and writings. When eleven years old, his father went to take charge of the living of Clovelly, where the boy was introduced to the shifting scenes of a busy coast life, and his young mind filled with all the picturesque details of a sea-roving population. Here he learned to esteem those manly qualities, and here, perhaps, he caught the spirit of adventure which he noted in the rugged sons of the sea who inhabit the Cornish coast. Here, too, he acquired that love for the common people in their natural dignity, brought up as he was in close contact with them, as we may see by reading between the lines his description of them in *Two Years Ago*. Here he acquired that personal popularity which stood him in good stead afterwards when dealing with Chartists and popular leaders. It was not only the result of natural-ness and innate *bonhommie*, but the effect of having lived among the people and understanding their ways. That tact and sympathetic intelligence which inspires popular confidence is best taught by living among the people, though not of them, in early life, before the full consciousness of social demarcation and the differences of rank and fortune become a bar to free and easy intercourse. Kingsley had the additional advan-tage of being the son of a clergyman, as he says himself

in a letter to a clergyman, and in answer to some
strictures on *Alton Locke*—

"From my cradle, as the son of an active clergyman, I
have been brought up in the most familiar intercourse with
the poor in town and country. My mother, a second Mrs.
Fry, in spirit and act. For fourteen years my father has
been the rector of a very large metropolitan parish, and I
speak what I know, and testify that which I have seen."

What the effect of these congenital tendencies and
early experiences were on the character of the boy, and
how far in his case the child proved to be the father of
the man, may be gathered from a few incidents of early
life, and a few scattered fragments of early thoughts
preserved in the Life we possess by his own wife.
Impulsiveness, precocity, conscientious susceptibility,
shyness and eccentricity seem to have been his main
characteristics in childhood. "*Don't cant*, Elizabeth!"
he says when six years old to a housemaid, condoling
with him on the occasion of a quarrel with his mother.
"Don't cant!" was the burden of his cry throughout
the whole extent of his mature life.

A similar rough, reprimanding, John the Baptist tone
runs through most of the sayings of "Parson Lot," with
an underground grunt of indignant objurgation against
social and religious pharisaisms more Gothic than
Hebraistic in their rigour. We note, too, in the child
something of the melancholy temperament peculiar to
the period of childhood in men who become famous in
after life, as a prelude of those later broodings over the
deeper problems of life which may be discovered alike

in such unlike persons as Goethe, J. S. Mill, and Lamennais. There is something of this serious and sombre sadness in Kingsley's earliest attempts in poetry; the very title of one written when he was a youth of sixteen or seventeen speaks of deep dejection as the result of early speculation—*Hypotheses Hypochondriacæ*, where he speaks of his "brooding melancholy."

In *Psyche, a Rhapsody*, belonging to the same period, he breaks out into wailing on the lives led by the poor in cities, presages of those more definite complaints of social wrongs to be found in his maturer writings—

"Then she passed on in her weary way through ancient cities, where the wealth and the glory of the world were heaped, for a strange desire was on her to seek for love through things above and things below, until she should rest in it for ever.

"And she wandered on; and from some houses came forth the glare of lamps, and the noise of song and revelry; but with it curses and shouts of strife; and from others the moaning of anguish, and the shrieks of despair. . . .

"And she shuddered and turned away. . . ."

Five years before Charles Kingsley had penned the *Rhapsody*, he had witnessed strange things at Bristol during the riots. He was then a shy and timid boy of twelve or thirteen years of age, and the horror of the scenes then witnessed left a deep mark on his mind, as he says himself. The mob of Bristol was accounted then as the most notorious for fierceness in the country, and it was at the time roused to a paroxysm of passion by the appearance of Sir C. Wetherell, the most un-

popular man in all England, visiting the city as Recorder.
Groans and yells, hooting and hissing from the crowd
greeted him wherever he appeared, and the business of
the court had to be adjourned on account of these in-
terruptions. He barely escaped personal violence by
flight from the Mansion House in disguise, and troops
had to be sent for to quell the riot. The mob set fire
to some of the public buildings of the city, and the
Bishop's palace was entirely destroyed, the Cathedral
nearly sharing the same fate. With great difficulty,
and not without some shedding of blood, order was
restored.

In a work entitled *The Working-man's Way in the
World, being the Autobiography of a Journeyman Printer*,
published in 1844, we have the sober sentiments of a
workman of the period dwelling on these events, and,
what is remarkable as coming from this source, showing
the darker side of the picture reflecting unfavourably
on his own class, the writer speaks of the riots as
" hideous bacchanals, where Gorgon ugliness, matured
in the filth and squalor of Bristol's darkest dens, and
slums of slime and excrement, was in strict keeping
with the seething hell of riot and rapine around . . .
the saturnalia of robbery and license got up under the
pretence of liberty and reform." In a lecture delivered
by Kingsley in Bristol twenty-seven years after this
event, he tells us how it taught him his first lesson
in social science. He speaks of the dark figures
flitting to and fro across what seemed the mouth of
the pit, but which was in reality a prison in flames;

the central mass of fire as he saw it from a distance rising behind Brandon Hill, and a day or two afterwards, in close proximity, the ghastly row of corpses, or fragments of corpses, in front of the ruins of burnt buildings. "It is good for a man," he adds, "to be brought once at least in his life face to face with fact, ultimate fact, however horrible may be" these base facts of life in lower regions, and the base morality it breeds. More of this he saw in later life, and describes, to show how the " dangerous classes " and the " dangers of society " arise from natural causes in the condition of things when the "better classes" neglect their social duty; what things may happen when greed and grasping selfishness and heartless self-indulgence in the classes above bring out the tiger and the beast in those below—social revolts being neither more nor less than a reverting to a former type of social co-existence, where the elemental strife and struggle for existence prevails, unmitigated by the higher forces of civilization. "One day," relates Mr. John Martineau, in a letter to Mrs. Kingsley, printed in the *Letters and Memories*, "as he was reading with me, something led him to tell me of the Bristol riots in 1832. He was in that year a school-boy of thirteen, at Bristol, and had slipped away, fascinated by the tumult and the horror, into the midst of it. He described— rapidly pacing up and down the room, and with glowing, saddened face, as though the sight was still before his eyes—the brave, patient soldiers, sitting hour after hour motionless on their horses, the blood streaming from wounds on their heads and faces, waiting for the

Bristol Riots 1832

order which the miserable, terrified Mayor had not courage to give; the savage, brutal, hideous mob of inhuman wretches, plundering, destroying, burning; casks of spirit broken open, and set flowing in the streets, the wretched creatures drinking it on their knees from the gutter, till the flames from a burning house caught the stream, ran down it with a horrible rushing sound, and, in one dreadful moment, the prostrate drunkards had become a row of blackened corpses. Lastly, he spoke of the shamelessness and the impurity of the guilty, the persecution and the suicide of the innocent.

"'That sight,' he said, suddenly turning to me, 'made me a Radical.'

"'Whose fault is it,' I ventured to ask, 'that such things can be?'

"'Mine,' he said, 'and yours.'

"I understood partly then, I have understood better now, what his radicalism was."

The effect on an emotional and excitable nature like Kingsley's was both instantaneous and indelible, a photograph imprinted on the mind to become an ever-present image, like the figure or sketch in the studio of the artist catching the eye at times, and unconsciously directing the hand as it works at his own creation, and giving colour to the picture of his own imagination.

When Kingsley's father removed to Chelsea in 1836, as rector of St. Luke's parish, another and by no means favourable view of social and clerical life presented itself to the son's mind. He is disgusted with the narrow conventionalities of middle-class respectability, and the hollowness of religious professions as then in vogue, and the paltriness of religious polemics, the reiteration of inane commonplaces, and the round of duties performed with puny egotism by the clerics and the clerically-minded lay-workers with whom he was brought into contact. His soul loathed much "the dapper young lady preachers" who visit the poor and read the Bible to them in " the most abominable scenes of filth, wretchedness, and indecency." The young ladies might have done worse, we think, and young Kingsley is rather too hard upon them, "falling in love with the preacher rather than the sermon," which is a practice not only of young women, but some old women of both sexes. We may imagine how Kingsley, a youth of seventeen, disgusted with the sight of these humdrum performances of " Church work," would turn to his Plato, which, his tutor at King's College, London, tells us, influenced much his mind at this period of his life, an influence, it may be inferred from his choice of Plato's works as a prize essay at Cambridge, continued long afterwards. Like most modern men of mark in the study of social and economic questions, Kingsley had to pass through a period of scepticism, a fact which it is not difficult to account for. Honest doubt is a characteristic of deeper minds, which are not easily satisfied with either the logical inconsequences of easy-going theological orthodoxy or the rank platitudes of social optimism. Eager souls are not as easily satisfied in their search after truth and social happiness

c

as the sluggish in temperament and the slow in imagination and intellectual grasp. The excitable temper of a highly nervous nature quickly perceives flaws in argument, and with the rapidity of sympathetic insight notices faults in social arrangements which leave the average man indifferent to the sorrows and sufferings of toiling humanity. Kingsley belonged to the former class. He conquered his doubts as he did most things, in a manly fashion, and lived to restore the faith of others who came to him for guidance. But what is more to our purpose in this sketch, he was thus enabled to cope with the difficulties of belief as they presented themselves to the minds of Chartists and Secularist leaders of the people with whom in after life he was thrown together, and over whom he thus exercised a most powerful influence. It is also curious to note that among the intellectual restoratives of his own beliefs were the works of Carlyle. In this, too, he showed the feelings of that generation of thinking young men, who, like his distinguished friend and future brother-in-law, Professor Froude, dissatisfied with the shallowness of prevailing make-beliefs, found in Carlyle a master who taught them to seek refuge in work whilst trying to combat their doubts. "Toil is the condition of our being," Kingsley writes to an Oxford friend from Cambridge in 1842; "our sentence is to labour from the cradle to the grave. But there are Sabbaths allowed for the mind as well as the body, when the intellect is stilled, and the emotions alone perform their gentle and involuntary function."

At this time, and in the interval between taking his degree and proceeding to his curacy, he began to write the life of St. Elizabeth of Hungary, the subject of the *Saint's Tragedy*, into which it was transformed a few years later.   When it is finished, he says he will begin the life of St. Theresa, to show the contrast between the working ascetic and the dreamy mystic, the celibate and married saint.   The two lives represent to him the social and religious aspects of the Christian's life on a high level which had now become Kingsley's Ideal.   In a similar way, a kindred mind, the Comte de Montalembert in France, approached the life of St. Elizabeth. To both it came as an inspiration to prepare them for their future labours in the cause of social and political reform on a Christian basis, respectively.   Thus the study of ideal characters and saintly lives attract the finer minds, and help in building up the spiritual system of souls, fitting them for the actualities of public life when the time has come for giving effect to ideal conceptions.   It may be matter of surprise to some why an ardent spirit like that of Kingsley was not at this time attracted, as were other gifted Cambridge men, by the Oxford Movement, which was a "movement for deeper religion, for a more real and earnest self-discipline, and a loftier morality, and more genuine self-devotion to a serious life."   The explanation is to be found mainly in his peculiar temperament, which in many respects was antipathetical to that of the men who set the movement a-going.   His excitable nature was repelled from their studious reserve and reticence, and their cautious, almost conscientious, abstinence from emotional religion and the exhibition of warmth of religious sentiment. They, like him, were intense, but repressed sternly the feelings which were too deep almost for expression. His impatience of trifles and proneness to inaccuracy in matters of detail, his hastiness in grasping at conclusions, his "impulsive and almost reckless generosity"—these and other characteristics naturally repelled him from the men who were the opposite of all this constitutionally, or by means of a self-determination on high grounds and severe discipline. He finds himself crying like a child as he listens to the tunes of some strolling fiddler under the window at Eversley, and though half ashamed of the emotion, he records it unblushingly in a letter to his future wife. Such a mobility of temperament was utterly at variance with the studied evenness of tone which was the early note of the leaders in the Oxford Movement. Besides this, Kingsley was opposed *toto cœlo* to their ascetic views of life. When the *Tracts for the Times* appeared, we are told he discussed them from the merely human, and not the religious point of view. He fiercely denounced the ascetic view of sacred human ties, sapping, as he thought, the very foundation of family and national life. His honest naturalness shrank from what appeared to him and many others at the time the "non-natural" sense of accepting religious truths, and the tortuous party methods which he criticized later in his controversy with Newman, but which, if it turned out a mistake, was so far important that it provoked the publication of the *Apologia*, the most remarkable book of this description in the English tongue.   Nurtured as Kingsley's mind had been by the theological speculations of Coleridge and F. D. Maurice, it had some affinities with the intellectual side of the movement.   For it was in one aspect, at least, a vigorous attempt to grapple intellectually with religious problems, to restore rationality and backbone to religious discussion.   None could sympathize more than he did with those men of the movement who like him were " talking strong " against the inane mediocrities of the day, defending the truths, as they called it, without being able to grasp in their feeble ineptitude the deeper problems of life and religion.   But Kingsley's conception of religion in its human as distinguished from its ecclesiastical aspect, gave him a leaning towards what was best in the Low Church party at this time, whose depth and subtlety of knowledge of the human heart he admired.   Both high and low have their good points, but " we must be catholic," he says, " without the partial or favourite views of Christianity, like the Dissenters and the Tractarians."

" Those who throw off humanity by lovelessness," he remarks elsewhere, " or Manicheism, seem to me, if they could succeed completely, beyond the pale of God's Church, which is the collective healthy humanity of the earth, and therefore beyond the pale of the spirit ! "

He called himself a mystic in theory and an ultra-materialist in practice, "the most prosaic and matter-of-fact of parsons," fishing, riding, hunting for beetles, and sometimes after other game, yet, he said once to his curate, "I am nothing if not a priest." The fact is, he had, as the latter puts it, a certain ideal of his own as to personal holiness and Church regimen which left him "a free lance in the ecclesiastical field." His Broad Church opinions were a refuge from the more narrow conceptions of Evangelicalism and Sacerdotalism alike. He was ready to accept whatever good there was in either. (But he felt that both lacked the one thing which he felt was needful for the time, a deep sense of the importance of religion in its social bearings.) Moreover he had in him, both as a child of nature and a naturalist, a form of natural religion and a dash of Wordsworthian nature-worship.

Thus when he wanders about in his parish in the bright July sun shortly after settling down to work in Eversley, and takes one of his lonely woodland baths, as he called it, this suggests to him, he naïvely states, thoughts of Paradise. "I know not," he says, "whether they are foretastes of the simple bliss that shall be in the renovated earth, or whether they are back glimpses into the former ages, when we wandered beside the ocean of eternal love!" Then after an apposite quotation from the ode on the *Intimations of Immortality*, he refers to the sermon of J. H. Newman on Reverence, as if in mind comparing his own nature-worship with the severe tone of a high-strung supra-natural devoutness in the great leader of the Tractarians, and remarks—" I was frightened at a sermon of Newman's on ' Christian Reverence,' in which he tries to show that Christ used to ' deter' people and *repel* them." But he adds further on, " Talking of the Tractators—so you still like their *tone !* and so do I. There is a solemn and gentlemanlike and gentle earnestness which is most beautiful, and which I wish I may ever attain." But he has no sympathy with " the moaning piety and something darker " in their writings. Yet, in a letter dated 1868, he speaks of the *Dream of Gerontius*, which he has just read, " with awe and admiration," and is glad that the man has appeared to teach our generation a sense of reverence which it is in danger of losing. The severe sternness with which the younger Kingsley could not readily sympathize was, as he felt later on, a tonic sadly needed at the time to restore a healthy vigour to the flabbiness of the religious nerves and muscles, to send a current of spiritual force through the system of National Religion, to restore a higher sense of sacredness of Divine things among a generation given to sanctimonious dallying and dawdling. Such was his own reverence and high tone in the performance of sacred functions, that a gentleman of the Press threatened to remove his son from Wellington College after attending College chapel where Kingsley was officiating on this occasion, because of his " high doctrine," a story vouched for by the present Archbishop of Canterbury, then head of the College.

What might have happened if the Oxford Movement

and the Christian Socialist movement had joined hands, and what impulse such a union of effort might have given to the social and religious reform which the country needed at the time, it is impossible to imagine. "Newman, too," we are told in the history of the Oxford Movement by Dean Church, lately published, " had laid down that the Church must rest on the people, and Froude looked forward to colleges of unmarried priests as the true way to evangelize the crowds." And, again, that as to Newman's sermons at St. Mary's, " what they aspired to revive and save, was the life of religion, the truth and substance of all that makes it *the hope of human society.*" But the times were un-favourable to such a confluence of the streams of religious and social movement, and a coalescence of high and noble aims in their differently and diversely constituted and gifted promoters.

The air was charged with religious controversy. Kingsley speaks of himself as an " Ishmael of Catho-licity," and complains of the state of religious opinion as the " salt asphaltic lake of polemics "—Popery and Puritanism fighting their battle over again in England on " the foul middle-ground of Mammonite infidelity." He longs for a new Order of St. Francis, a brotherhood of religious genius to cope with our social difficulties. For parsons have degenerated into a body of rural police in the country, and the Church has become an ecclesiastical system unable to meet the spiritual needs of a rioting democracy in the towns. He sees the finger on the wall writing its " ' *mene, mene* ' against

Anglicanism and Evangelicalism at once—both of which more and more daily prove to me their utter impotence to meet our social evils." . . . "In plain truth, the English clergy must Arnold-ize, if they do not wish to go either to Rome or to the workhouse before fifty years are out. There is, I do believe, an Arnold-ite spirit rising; but most *laudant, non sequuntur*. Decent Anglicanism, decent Evangelical Conservatism (or Evangelicanism) having become the majority, is now quite Conservative, and each party playing Canute and the tide, as it can scramble in turn into the chair of authority." That in all this Kingsley in no way exaggerated the state of things, may be seen from what appears in the recorded sayings and writings of working-men leaders and the mouthpieces of popular discontent at the time. Here we see the most forcible strictures of popular religion expressed in a tone of sad and sincere regret, and coupled with touching appeals to the representatives of the National Church to rise to the occasion, and to apply once more the force of religion as a spiritual leverage power for the elevation of the people. Thus William Lovett reminds religious people of this surpassing importance of duty as distinguished from doctrine in matters of religion, of conduct as more important than mere convictions which the religious world then thought all-important.

"When our religious convictions are based on *duty*, when we are clearly led to perceive that a certain and conscientious *course of conduct* is necessary to be observed

by every individual in this world to secure individual
happiness and human well-being, we have a hopeful and
stable religion, urging us from day to day, and from year
to year, to our best efforts for the enlightenment, moral
elevation, and general improvement of humanity."

And after dwelling on the futility of great reverence for
religion in theory in the bishops and clergy and religious
people generally, whilst neglecting its practical application to the duty of the individual and social life—

" Remember that the highest *Christian duty*, the highest
moral duty, as well as the highest of our *political duties*,
all point to the same great end—that of improving and
perfecting our fellow-creatures intellectually, morally, and
physically, so that they may be enabled to enjoy the highest
amount of happiness in this world, and be the better
prepared for the enjoyment of the next." [1]

From such expressions we may learn what warmed
really the spirit of such a man as Kingsley to something
like fever-heat. The plot is thickening, as Kingsley calls
it, with " the poor Church of England, the clergy busy
with their commenting and squabbling and doctrine-
picking, while the world of labour turned away from
the Church with disgust." Things came to a head in
1848. He had been watching the rising tide of Chartism in his own parish. He had done his best, had
preached to the people on the subjects of the day, on
emigration, poaching, and the political and social disturbances of the hour. Now he felt he must join his

[1] *The Life and Struggles of William Lovett, in his pursuit of
Bread, Knowledge, and Freedom.* London, 1876, pp. 383-5, 435,
and *passim.*

friends in London and take his share in the work of
quelling the storm.   His utterances in this first essay of
coping with the question are supposed to have been
very *outré*, and are excused by some of his friendly
critics and apologists, defended on the ground that he
lost his head a little in the first blush of the general
excitement.   We cannot see anything of the kind in
the sayings and writings of the period to justify this
line of defence.   We note, on the contrary, a wonderful
amount of calm judgment considering the man's
character and the state of the public mind at the
moment.   It is his critics who at the time lost their
heads, not he, in their formidable fear of the dangers
with which they supposed society was threatened.   He,
braced up by years of quiet repose and communings
with nature in his country retreat, keeping sufficiently
in touch with the intellectual and social movement
throughout the country, by means of correspondence
and personal intercourse with his London friends, was
well equipped to form a judgment on the state of
affairs, better at least than those who lived in the
whirlpool of excitement.   This comes out in one of the
papers to Chartists, which he wrote for *Politics of the
People*, specially addressed to the Chartists at the time.
Its subject is the British Museum, which he calls "a
true, equalizing place, in the deepest and most spiritual
sense," and then goes on to show how in the higher and
ideal enjoyments of man all are equal; how the poorest
journeyman contributing cheerfully his mite to the
palace of Art in the National Museum stands on the

same platform with the wealthiest contributor to such
national institutions, and accordingly may claim the
same right to enjoy the noble treasures there stored up.
He adds: "I never felt this more strongly than some six
months ago, as I was looking in at the windows of a
splendid curiosity shop in Oxford Street, at a case of
humming-birds. I was gloating over the beauty of
these feathered jewels, and then wondering what was
the meaning, what was the use of it all. . . . Next me
stood a huge, brawny coalheaver, in his shovel-hat and
white stocks and highlows, gazing at the humming-
birds as earnestly as myself. As I turned he turned,
and I saw a bright, manly face, with a broad, soot-
grimed forehead, from under which a pair of keen
flashing eyes gleamed wondering, smiling sympathy into
mine. In that moment we felt ourselves to be friends.
. . . I never felt more thoroughly than at that minute
(though, thank God, I had often felt it before) that all
men were brothers; that fraternity and equality were
not mere political doctrines, but blessed, God-ordained
facts; that the party walls of rank and fashion and
money were but a paper prison of our own making,
which we might break through any moment by a
single hearty and kindly feeling; that the one Spirit
of God was given without respect of persons; that
the beautiful things were beautiful alike to the coalheaver and the parson; and that before the wondrous
works of God, and of God-inspired genius, the rich
and the poor might meet together, and feel that whatever the coat or the creed may be, 'A man's a man for

a' that,' and one Lord the maker of them all." And then the clenching argument founded on all this: "For believe me, my friends, rich and poor—and I beseech you to think deeply over this great truth—that men will never be joined in true brotherhood by mere plans to give them a self-interest in common, as the Socialists have tried to do. No : to feel *for* each other they must first feel *like* each other. To have their sympathies in common, they must have not one object of gain, but an object of admiration in common ; to know that they were brothers, they must feel that they have one Father; and a way to feel that they have one common Father, is to see each other wondering side by side at His glorious works."

Not all his utterances reach this high level of serene impartiality and unclouded vision in the rarefied region of true social philosophy. He himself describes his own state of mind at this time as chaotic, piecemeal, passionate ; he feels like the " wild man of the woods," who cannot speak the truth without disturbing in his own soul "a hornet-swarm of lies." But it is a Divine mania which has taken hold of him; it is " the word of the Lord like fire in my bones." But his self-depreciation must not be taken too seriously. One thing is certain, the Chartists thought him mealy-mouthed like the rest of his cloth. He is wounded when they and their clients approach him with suspicion. He gives expression to this in a letter to Thomas Cooper, after reading the latter's poem, *The Purgatory of Suicides*, and appealing to a poet's sympathy to understand him better than the rest. "Just because I am a clergyman," he says, "the very office which *ought* to have testified above all others for liberty, equality, brotherhood, for time and eternity," becomes the occasion of distrust. " I felt myself bound, then, to write to you, to see if among the nobler spirits of the working-classes I could not make one friend who would understand me . . . I would shed the last drop of my life-blood for the social and political emancipation of the people of England. . . . I want to work with them ; I want to realize my brotherhood with them. I want some one like yourself, intimately acquainted with the mind of the working-classes, to give me such an insight into their life and thoughts as may enable me to consecrate my powers effectually to their service."

His health broke down under the pressure of work and excitement, and he had to seek rest at Ilfracombe. Before returning thence to his parish he goes to London to attend again Chartist meetings, and meetings in connection with land colonization and the association of tailors. He is delighted to discover by this time that his village sermons are lent from hand to hand among the South London Chartists, and that the Manchester men actually stole a copy of the *Saint's Tragedy*—a sign of their better understanding of his sympathies with their cause. The old spirit is upon him again ; we see it from the manner in which he describes his master at the business meeting of this Tailors' Association. " Last night," he writes June 12th, 1849, "will never be forgotten by many, many men. Maurice was—I cannot describe it. Chartists told me this morning that many were affected even to tears. The man was inspired—prophetic. No one commented on what he said. He stunned us! I will tell you when I can collect myself."

And with this impression on his mind as to the magnitude of the task before them, and the magnanimity of the man who led them to discharge it, he returns to Eversley. His life there, as a country parson, as the minister of reconciliation in things sacred and social, engaged in the literary labours which quickly established his fame, and how far some of them helped to popularize the movement, will be described in the next and following chapters.

CHAPTER II.

KINGSLEY AS COUNTRY PARSON—EVERSLEY HOME-
LIFE AND PAROCHIAL LABOURS.

In 1842 Kingsley took charge of the curacy of
Eversley, to which he was appointed as Rector two
years later, and where he spent thirty-three years of his
life. Here, remarks one who knew him intimately
in this beautiful home-scene and truly ideal English
Rectory, was "the fountain-head of all his strength and
greatness." The surrounding scenery though lovely is
not exciting. With acacias on the lawn, a glimpse of
the fir forest and moors at a distance, the old Windsor
forest forming part of the parish boundaries, there was
just enough and not too much in the environment to
inspire a quiet and young parish priest in his labours.
The people among whom he was to minister were
"heth-croppers," and, we are told, poachers by instinct,
and there is a curiously half disguised sympathy with
poachers in the poems written about this time. How
quickly Kingsley caught the spirit of his surroundings,
and learned to assimilate his nature and identify his
own instincts with those of the people whose spiritual

director he had become, may be seen in a passage taken from the *Prose Idylls,* and quoted in the Letters and Memories of his Life.

" The clod of these parts is the descendant of many generations of broom squires and deer-stealers ; the instinct of sport is strong within him still, though no more of the Queen's deer are to be shot in the winter turnip-fields, or even caught by an apple-baited hook hung from an orchard bough. He now limits his aspirations to hares and pheasants, and too probably once in his life 'hits the keeper into the river,' and re-considers himself for awhile over a crank in Winchester gaol. Well, he has his faults, and I have mine. But he is a thorough good fellow, nevertheless ; civil, contented, industrious, and often very handsome, a far shrewder fellow, too—owing to his dash of wild forest blood, from gipsy highwaymen, and what not— than his bullet-headed and flaxen-polled cousin, the poor south Saxon of the chalk downs. Dark-haired he is, ruddy, and tall of bone, swaggering in his youth ; but when he grows old, a thin gentleman, reserved, stately, and courteous as a prince."

With such a fund of sympathetic intelligence in descrying the character of his people, and accordingly adapting himself, as he says somewhere, "trying to catch men by *their* leading ideas, and so draw them off insensibly to *my* leading ideas," he gains respect and affection. Found to be by these wild young fellows neither a "young Methodist" nor an "effeminate ascetic," "they dare not gainsay, but rather look up to a man who they see is their superior, if he choose to exert his power in physical as well as intellectual skill." And this we are told was the secret of his influence

D

and success in Eversley. He could discuss the rotation
of crops with the farmers, and understood hedging and
ditching as well as the labourer. He could swing a
flail and pitch hay as well as the best of them, nor was
he surpassed by a sportsman all the country round for
his knowledge and skill as a fisherman or a huntsman,
yet he is the clergyman all the same, and whilst using
these subsidiary means for ingratiating himself with his
parishioners, he does so because they are auxiliary to
higher ends. The parish had been badly neglected
before he came, and he sets to work at once to redeem
it "from barbarism," and the evil effects of pauperism.
"I am trying in my way to do good; but what is the
use of talking to hungry paupers about heaven? 'Sir,' as
my clerk said to me yesterday, 'there is a weight upon
their hearts, and they care for no hope and no change,
for they know they can be no worse off than they are.'
And so they have no spirit to arise, and go to their
Father. Those who lounge upon down beds, and
throw away thousands at Crockford's and Almack's—
they, the refined of this earth, have crushed it out of
them. I have been very sad lately, seeing this, and
seeing, too, the horrid effects of that new Poor Law."
The man who felt like this and looked into the condition-
of-the-people question with clear eyes, would naturally
attract toward his person, and influence by his teaching
the people of his parish, whose trials he so well understood, and helped to bear. Everybody knew and loved
him for his naturalness and perfect ease. There was
a perfectly good understanding between minister and

people. He really respected the poor, as all will who
know them intimately; he revered them in their heroic
struggles and innate kindliness, there was the same
chivalric courtesy and consideration for them as for
all the rest, and there was no artificiality in it. He
resembled the ideal country parson drawn by Wordsworth, as probably he is, or was then, more common in
Scotland than in England.

> "Man he loved
> As man ; and, to the mean and the obscure
> And all the homely in their homely works,
> Transferr'd a courtesy which had no air
> Of condescension."

Of course he set in motion the whole machinery
of ordinary parish institutions on a more extensive
scale even than that of the well-organized parish
of the present day, a very unusual thing in the best
of country parishes then. Clubs, schools, maternal
society, loan fund, lending library, adult evening classes
held three times in the week at the Rectory before
through his exertion the school-room was built, village
lectures, singing classes for adults to introduce Church
music on Hullah's plan to supersede the instrumental
music of trombone and clarionet, and much besides.
In other things he not only equalled but excelled
in self-sacrificing energy and effort the earnest country
parson. There was no lack of earnestness and zeal
in the ordinary routine of parochial work, though there
was a complete and wholesome absence of the stiff and
starched clerical officialism which mars the honest

work of many a good clergyman who is too much of the cleric and too little of the man. Besides this Kingsley somehow found time for a multiplicity of other important engagements, literary and tutorial, as well as for simple and healthy enjoyments in field and forest, stream and mountain, for which others have neither the capacity nor the will, but which vastly added to his own usefulness. His good-humour and love of fun and frolic endeared him to all with whom he came into contact, and it helped him considerably to make life tolerable and happy in his country retreat.

In a letter written in the first year at Eversley and signed humorously "Boanerges Roar-at-the-Clods," he invites a friend to come and cheer up his loneliness. Peter comes and sees him living in a thatched cottage, but, as he remarks, as happy as if it had been a palace, and cheerful withal notwithstanding the monotony of the daily task. Nor in after life at any time does he express any desire to leave the simple village. He found the monotony "pleasant in itself, morally pleasant and morally useful," as he puts it, and we may add intellectually fruitful. Here in the heart of the country and amid the occupations of rural life he found the calming and healthily stimulating and never exciting influences to steady and brace his susceptible mind for his best work. *Yeast* and *Alton Locke* might have lost little if Kingsley had composed them amid the stirring life of towns. But the *Saint's Tragedy*, *Hypatia*, and the most finished productions of his pen, not excluding his more important contributions to the Christian socialist publications, were the better for his life in comparative retirement. He seldom went to London, and when a friend pressed him to come up and hear one of his own songs finely sung in public, he refused. "I love home and green fields more and more, and never lust either after Babylon or the Continent." A quick intelligence, like Kingsley's, readily followed the movements in the world beyond his own church steeple, and there was little in the current of events which escaped his notice. The fact is, the true nature and tendency of the more prominent movements in society and the current of events can be watched with a closer scrutiny and more intelligent interest from a distance and a permanent standpoint, such as life in the country affords, than by an observer placed in the midst of the shifting scenes and turmoil of town life, especially if the observer be a man of Kingsley's excitable temperament.

Nor is a country parson's life as uneventful as some imagine, especially if, like Charles Kingsley, he is ever on the alert to see the significance of events, and to turn them to spiritual profit. Thus, when the cholera broke out in his own parish, he does not take simply precautions to seal the Rectory hermetically against infection, and to improve the occasion on Sundays by preaching sermons full of "precautionary piety," teaching his people to think of the uncertainty of life and to prepare for that which is to come ; but himself ubiquitous in his parish, a true parish priest, like Aaron standing between the living and the dead, he inculcates from the pulpit the duty of sanitary precaution to save life, and varies his parochial work by laying out plans for draining the parish at those points where low fever had prevailed, and, moreover, engaged in a crusade against dirt and bad drainage elsewhere by speech and pen. So, again, when diphtheria breaks out in Eversley, he disregards the great duty of self-preservation, and runs at the risk of his own life and that of his dear ones from cottage to cottage with bottles of gargle and other medicaments to prevent the progress of the disease. Again, when a great heath fire breaks out among the flats, even if it happens in the middle of Divine Service, the Rector is seen actually rushing out of church, leaving the curate to finish the service, whilst he sallies forth armed with bill-hook, organizing bands of beaters, going forth, himself among the rest, to resist the further advance of the flames, and during the night going round to inspect the country and cheering the watchers, and so preserving the firs he loved so much from being consumed by fire. Thus, as Mr. C. Kegan Paul puts it, Kingsley, "with a twenty-parson power," though unlike the ordinary conventional parson in most respects, managed to administer his parish so ably, to read with his pupils, to write his books, to keep up a considerable correspondence, yet always having a considerable reserve of nervous tissue for interesting conversation, and for occasional fishing, riding, and walking. And all this with a physical frame powerful and wiry indeed, but having the seeds of decay which shortened his life. It shows how much may be done by a wise economy of labour, and avoidance of frittering away the best hours of the day by what the French term *choses pour rien dire.* How he managed it may be seen from the agenda of a single day as sketched by his wife, referring to his work in the winter of 1850. He rose every morning at five, and wrote till breakfast. He then worked with his pupils and at his sermons. In the afternoons he visited the people; the evenings were occupied in teaching the adult school and superintending the fair copy of *Alton Locke* made by his wife. In his walks, or at the trout-stream, or engaged in any out-door occupations he would think out most of the thoughts committed to writing, mostly by dictation, afterwards. Sometimes when pressed for time he would write during the greater part of the night after everybody had gone to rest. Thus, as will be seen, he lost little time, and crowded much work into a comparatively short but "highly vital life," as Bishop Wilberforce calls it in a letter addressed to Kingsley in 1869, containing the compliment, which coming from such a source adds the stamp of orthodoxy on his life and labours: "I am quite certain of your powers being used on the side of that truth which so many, as it seems to me, in their way longing to support it, distrust and dishonour." The restlessness of Kingsley's mind prevented him from coming under that dreadful bane of even the gifted country parson, namely, intellectual immobility or retarded intellectual development, because all things round him move

so slowly, and the discharge of his simple duties is
apt to generate perfunctoriness in their performance,
and a relapse into learned or it may be unlearned
ease. His case is an instance to point a comforting
lesson to the friends and relatives of "able" young
men, for whom they are in constant fear lest they
should be "lost in the country." As a safe and sound
fulcrum for a wider influence, Kingsley's position in
the country was of much value. Mr. J. Martineau
bears testimony to this in a letter to Mrs. Kingsley
giving his recollections of him—

"As it was an unspeakable blessing to Eversley to have
him for its Rector, so also it was an inestimable benefit to
him to have had so early in life a definite work to do
which gave to his generous sympathetic impulses abundant
objects and responsibilities, and a clearer purpose and
direction. Conscious, too, as he could not but be, of great
powers, and impatient of dictation and control, the repose
and isolation of a country parish afforded him the best and
healthiest opportunities of development, and full liberty of
thought and speech, with sufficient leisure for reading and
study."

Besides this, the truly able clergyman makes every
event and circumstance and act, unimportant to
ordinary persons or parsons, significant and interesting
by the reality he gives to it, and raising it by his
own innate elevation of tone to a higher level. Club-
day in a country district is a kind of holiday, important
to those concerned in it, but to the eye of the outsider
presenting little interest, having even an air about it
of the ludicrous in the exhibition of antiquated forms

of a would-be grand paraphernalia, and the quaint
titles of the chief office-bearers not always supported
by corresponding dignity in person and bearing.
Kingsley sees the kernel of which these are only the
outward shell. He preaches to the people assembled in
the church on that verse of the twelfth chapter of the
Corinthians, in which the Church is represented as an
association, with its spiritual force and functions dis-
tributed on a unifying principle ; shows how the world as
it is, is a "selfish competitive isolating form of society,"
and holds up the social ideal of the Church, in which
diverse powers differently used contribute to the common
end ; shows how the early Christians had all things in
common in accordance with this principle, i. e. "the
uniting socialist one"—socialist, that is, as opposed
to selfish individualism—and leads the minds of his
hearers on to what he calls the millennium, the kingdom of God a perfect society here on earth. Thus
he hallows the occasion, and lifts the minds of his
hearers out of the region of commonplace reflection
to something higher and better. In the letter which
records this fact he speaks of his occupation during this
Whitsun-week. On Friday he goes a-fishing, but the
perch will not bite. Then goes to see E. H. to read
and pray with her. On this he remarks, "How one
gets to love consumptive patients! She seems in a
most happy, holy state of mind, thanks to Smith" (the
curate). He sees another patient, and sits a long time
with her. Then he goes to look up John, who had had
bad luck in fishing, hooking a huge jack, which broke

everything in a moment, and went off with all his spinning-tackle. They were caught in a storm, which Kingsley describes with his realistic intensity, not omitting to state how he prayed when he saw the danger they were in. Then follows a vivid account of birds nesting, and an inventory of his treasures reserved for hen and chicks, and so forth. In all this we have the man exactly as he is, a strange mixture of earnestness and fun, deep reverence and rollicking cheerfulness, serious without falsity or affectation, bright and brimful with high spirits, yet with a real sanctity visible in all he does and says, without a shadow of sanctimoniousness, varying his occupations from grave to gay without losing his moral equilibrium, work and relaxation alternating with each other to keep up the intellectual balance. Only on rare occasions he gives way to a momentary feeling of weariness arising from over-exertion and exhaustion, when—and this more towards the close of his life—he says at times to his wife, " How blessed it will be when it is all over ! "

It will not be out of place here to say a few words on Kingsley in his own parish church ; of the Rector surrounded by visitors on the lawn ; of the man in his home life and the circle of his family and intimates, to show how well he succeeds in that peculiar mission of the country parson, civilizing, enlightening, elevating, energizing rural life, and raising it above the low level of mental dulness and grovelling care into a nobler and more fruitful existence. The present taste for

biographical sketches of the personal and home life of
celebrated men and women is not altogether a bad sign
of the times. People desire to know whether the man
whose public work they admire so much is really what
he seems to be in his writings, what are his personal
habits and his life at home, for there have been cases
of social philanthropists, and even religious reformers,
who deserved the epithet, "A devil at home, and a saint
abroad." The power of moral tension demanded in
private virtues is much greater than what will suffice
in the exhibition of public beneficence, because it is
constantly called into requisition and under constant
observation. Kingsley's life in the small area circum-
scribed by the parish boundaries, bears inspection. The
man and the social missionary, the writer and the
person who wrote, were all of one piece, and cast in
one mould. What struck those who watched him in
the regular performance of his ecclesiastical functions in
the church at Eversley, was the unprofessional sincerity
of his devoutness, the loyal and loving rendering of the
Church services without the slightest accretion of would-
be pious attitudinizing, or over-studious attention to
ritualistic detail, that kind of scrupulous and punctilious
carefulness in gesture and movement which lessens
rather than increases the solemnity of worship, and
tends to magnify the officiating priest rather than the
Creator and Preserver of all mankind. As to his teaching,
he accepted *ex animo*, and without mental reservation,
the teaching of the Church to which he belonged, avoiding conscientiously the vagaries of Broad Churchism, as

well as those of the High and Low Churchmanship. To accept anything in the formularies in what Mr. Ward called a "non-natural sense," was simply impossible to a man of such transparent naturalness as Kingsley. To express unnatural feelings, so as to arouse the religious emotions in others, would to him have been as impossible as seeing its display in others would have been to him a loathing sight. For this reason the present Archbishop, as Chancellor Benson and head of the Lincoln Theological School, held up Kingsley as a pattern for young clergymen. " I never did," he says, in his letter to Mrs. Kingsley, "and I believe I never shall, see anything that spoke so loud for the Church of England as never to be put away, as did the morning service in Eversley Church, whether he read or preached."

It is a long way from an archbishop to a curate ; but curates—and every curate is a potential archbishop— can be severe critics at times ; we would quote, therefore, the impressions made on the mind of one of Kingsley's curates by way of contrast. After describing how, one Sunday morning, the Rector walking from the altar to the pulpit suddenly disappeared, owing to the fact, as was afterwards discovered, that *en route* a lame butterfly arrested his attention, and which accordingly he conveyed to the vestry as a place of refuge *pro tem.*, he goes on to compare his village to his town sermons, and remarks : " To my mind, he was never heard to greater advantage than in his own village pulpit. I have sometimes been so moved by what he then said, that I could scarcely restrain myself from calling out,

as he poured forth words, now exquisitely sad and
tender, now grand and heroic, with an insight into
character, a knowledge of the world, and a sustained
eloquence which, each in its own way, were matchless."

In the manner of preaching we note the same characteristics of complete unconventionality, the ring of
artless sincerity, transparent truthfulness, telling directness of speech and definiteness of thought, never too
deep, and never approaching shallowness, a style always
plain and never bald, original in the sense of not being
a repetition of commonplaces, which made the spoken
word powerful, because it came from the inner depths
of the man himself. His sermons, short, pithy, unpre-
tentious, have the merit above all things of what Mr.
Matthew Arnold would call lucidity. They are clear
with the clearness of a narrow trout-stream such as
his soul loved, but not to be compared with the
breadth and depth of the ocean of thought such as we
look for in the sermons of Robertson or Newman. We
can understand how the poor men in the free sittings
would settle themselves into an attitude of attention,
as we are told they did as soon as he gave out his text,
and how in preaching he would try, but ineffectually,
to maintain calmness, his eager intensity and power of
emotional force within him gaining the mastery over
him; his eyes aflame, his wiry frame vibrating with
terrible earnestness, as he delivered his message here in
the dimly-lit and sparsely-attended church. During the
evenings in Passion Week he would exhibit the same
solemn tone and look of inspiration, overpowered by

the subject, and forgetting the surroundings, damping enough to the ordinary preacher—a sure sign of depth of feeling and self-forgetful enthusiasm, thus unsustained by the real or supposed sympathetic rebound of feeling from a large assembly of appreciative hearers. To this quality of spiritual force in the man and his message, must be ascribed the power of his sermons and their immediate effect, and also in a secondary manner on those who read them in their published form. A clergyman, working in an important city parish, speaks of the twenty-five village sermons as "a plank to a drowning man," which "kept me from sinking in the ' blackness of darkness' which surrounds the unbeliever. Leaning upon these, while, carried about by every wind of doctrine, I drifted hither and thither, at last, thanks be to God, I found standing-ground."

We have read a number of them and other published sermons of Kingsley's, preached on different occasions and in a variety of places, including the Westminster sermons among the rest, with a view to discover the secret of their power and popularity. But, to be perfectly candid, much as we feel inclined to pass a favourable dictum, much as we admire the ease of diction, the shrewd common sense, the charm of simplicity which pervades them, the complete freedom from tedious circumlocution and turgid verbosity which spoils the sermons of even able but much-occupied men ; much, too, as we admire the undoubted eloquence of a number of passages here and there, specially as in the case of the sermon preached at Bideford on " Public Spirit," or the sermon on "Human Soot," preached in Liverpool, under the inspiration of the place and the congenial nature of the theme, we cannot, speaking critically, place these sermons in the first rank of pulpit oratory. What rendered them popular at the time was no doubt their utter unlikeness to the dreary sermons of the day delivered by scholarly and good men with all the droning dignity and somnolent solemnity of respectable Church of Englandism, and also their unlikeness to the highly-spiced, flashy, and inflammatory effusions of O'Blare-aways, the men of sound without sense of whom he gives a picture in *Yeast*, and who are so mercilessly held up to ridicule and contempt in the stories of Anthony Trollope and other painters of the clerical life of that time. It was refreshing at last to hear a man say exactly what he meant, and who meant something in what he said to his hearers; to listen to one who never affected what he did not feel, and who felt very deeply every word he said; a preacher whose aim was not to produce pleasant ripples of emotion in well-dressed, pious virgins, and waves of approval in severely critical dames, even those whom Robertson when in Cheltenham called his Muslin Episcopate, causing at the same time deep sleep to fall on the men, not, as in the case of Eliphaz the Temanite, accompanied by thrilling inspiration. In Kingsley's racy, manly village sermons there were no asides for the benefit of the cushioned pews, to show how the parson could lecture inferiors on their duties to the powers that be, including perhaps the Deity, but certainly not excluding the squire. As if acute villagers could not see through such a trick, and despise the parson accordingly, and justly so ! Nor were there here in these sermons the usual appeals in vogue at that time to selfish fears and debasing hopes. "You know," he said to a clergyman of our acquaintance who came to be interviewed as his future curate, "I don't allow swearing in my church." What he meant was, of course, he never would encourage denunciation against the guilty in the "old style," though he could hold up the stern aspect of religious truth when the occasion required it. Here, then, there were sermons free from conventional phrases and party passwords, without a painful attention to word-building, written as the ideas welled up in the heart, put into appropriate words, spontaneous, suggestive, informal; they had actuality, the very quality which was wanting mostly in the average sermon of the day. Freshness of treatment, truthfulness in utterance, a poet's quickness and perception in the use of tropes and illustrations, and a shrewd man's directness of aim, a power of seizing rapidly a few salient points, expressed in simple, well-selected words and phrases, distinguished by conciseness of form rather than completeness in substance, adapted to the power of attention in an average audience, which cannot bear the strain of close and prolonged reasoning, —such were the qualities of his discourses, qualities in themselves quite sufficient to gain for them a widely-enjoyed and well-earned popularity, enhanced by the fact that these sermons were preached by a man rendered famous by his other works, and certainly not diminished by Charles Kingsley's well-known acceptableness as a court preacher.

The parish itself after a time became the centre of attraction to many who either sympathized with the social aims or had become interested in the literary productions of the Rector. One of these was the Right Hon. Thomas Erskine, who came to reside in it, and soon became the friend and counsellor of Charles Kingsley. At his house, Fir Grove, Kingsley met many men of congenial minds, and formed some of the most important friendships of his life. Visitors, too, came to Eversley from many quarters, either drawn by curiosity or coming to receive counsel and advice: Americans, and among them a formidable rival as a writer of social fiction, Mrs. Beecher Stowe; philanthropists, and social and sanitary reformers nearer home, notably Mr. Chadwick, to mention one out of many. At the church on Sundays might be seen Crimean officers, who had come over from Sandhurst or Aldershot to hear the author of those stirring stories which had whiled away weary hours in field hospitals in strange lands whilst their wounds were healing. Other strangers came to fill the church during the summer months, a by no means unmingled source of gratification to the Rector, who often used to say, " I cannot bear having my place turned into a fair on Sundays, and all this talking after church." More congenial to his tastes were the talks on the lawn under the fir-trees, with a group of guests often including

E

men either famous at the time or become distinguished
since. It was a motley crowd of Churchmen and
Dissenters, Unitarian ministers and future Archbishops;
even Queen Emma of the Sandwich Islands came to
visit the author of the *Water Babies,* which her husband
had been reading to their young prince.

Letters, too, streamed in from various quarters when
personal intercourse was rendered impracticable, sometimes from unknown persons, as one signed " A Chartist
and a Cabman," thanking him for the pleasure derived
from *Alton Locke;* another from a barrister writing from
South Australia, thanking him for the comfort derived
from his sermons; one from a Wesleyan minister from
Grahamstown; from China; another from the other
side of the Rocky Mountains—in short, from all points
of the compass these missives came to assure him of
his wide influence. At the same time he corresponds
on subjects of scientific and literary interest with such
men as Darwin, Huxley, Matthew Arnold, and Lionel
Tollemache, not to mention a host of others. One feels
almost overwhelmed by the variety of subjects and the
versatility of a mind which could address itself to all
of them with intense interest, for his letters on these
different subjects invariably display a carefully-directed
attention to each point under discussion; they are not
replies written off in the eager rapidity which the
severity of strain on the minds of most men of note in
the present day almost renders an obligation; but they
are carefully-weighed and patiently-considered judg-
ments formed by a quick but thoroughly conscientious

mind. We might instance among them those letters on Strikes and Trades Unions, written in reply to questions put to him by his London friends, who, though writing themselves from the scene of action to one who lived far from it, could not help acknowledging the wisdom and good sense of his advice. If it be recollected, moreover, that all this while Kingsley has a multiplicity of other engagements, brain work of the highest order, and the multiplicity of small worries which take so much out of a man, however free from or able to conquer impending mental irritability, Kingsley never lost the cheerful tenor of his even temper, and the unfailing genial humour in his home-life and in contact with those around him. To his own children, and those of his friends, he was always the same bright, cheerful, light-hearted friend and playfellow. " I am staying near Kingsley with my wife and children," writes F. D. Maurice to Daniel Macmillan in 1852, "who love him almost as much as I do." Equally touching was his unfailing tenderness to his aged mother, brightening up her last years of failing health, always having a cheering word in her moments of depression, and equally touching attention to a delicate wife, forgetting or trying to forget his own hard work and worry in the interest of his family. "There he sat," says his son, " with one hand in mother's, forgetting his own hard work and worry in leading our fun and frolic, with a kindly smile on his lips, and a loving light in that bright eye that made us feel that in the broadest sense of the word he was our father." His curate, speaking of his own reminiscences of Kingsley's "heroism in home-life," tells the same story, and we have heard others who knew him in the intimacy of the home circle confirm the same impression, and one who by no means loved Kingsley as a man after his own heart, that he was never greater than at his own fireside. "Home was to him the sweetest, the fairest, the most romantic thing in life ; and there all that was best and brightest in him shone with steady and purest lustre."

The same cheerfulness of a loving temperament and affectionate thoughtfulness for others accompanied him in his walks through the parish ; it was the power of radiating warmth and light which drew all men towards him. The parish was near his heart at all times, and therefore all hearts were full of affection for him, though, of course, not all in the same degree ; but none could resist such genuine and perfectly natural love for his people as was that of the Rector of Eversley. He identified himself with Eversley, and when the enclosure of Eversley Common was decided upon it was a real distress to him. "Eversley will be no longer the same Eversley to me," he said with a pang. Immediately on his return from the American tour, though not yet recovered from his illness in Colorado, he throws himself into his parish work eagerly, glad to return to his simple parishioners, and in the prevalence of much sickness and mortality among them, visiting them twice and three times a day in a burning sun and dry easterly wind. One or two such facts are quite enough to show the relation of parson and people. There are excellent

men and conscientious, who, somehow, when placed in
country parishes, forfeit not only their ministerial, but
personal and social influence exactly from the want of
this common feeling, and the absence of anything like
a common interest between them and their parishioners.
They and their friends complain of the want of appreciation of their hard work and good intentions all thrown
away on people who cannot understand the purity of
their motives and excellence of their intentions. Not
so with Charles Kingsley. He did not think of himself,
and his dignity was never offended ; he thought and
lived for others, and so they thought well of him, and
loved him because they simply could not help it, and,
like his Master, " having loved his own, he loved them
to the end." For this reason he would never leave it
for any promotion except a canonry, which permitted
him to stay there. " Even a deanery I should shrink
from," he writes in 1869 to a friend congratulating him
on his appointment to a canonry at Chester ; " the home
to which I was ordained, where I came when I was
married, I intend shall be my last home : for go where
I will in this hard-working world, I shall take care to
get my last sleep in Eversley churchyard."

The angel of death made his appearance in the
Eversley home sooner than was expected. When for
the last time he returned to it from Westminster
Abbey in 1874, and his wife was taken seriously ill, so
much so that hopes of her recovery were abandoned, he
said, " My own death-warrant was signed with these
words." She recovered, but he was taken ill, and

though he made a "splendid fight for life," he suc-
cumbed, and the night came in which he said, "No
more fighting—no more fighting," and resignedly he
passed away.　Villagers, selected by himself on his death-
bed, carried him to his resting-place in the churchyard—those who had known, loved, and trusted him for
years.　The highest and lowest in the land stood round
that grave, representatives of every phase of life, because
the capacious mind and large-hearted soul of Charles
Kingsley had a sympathy which knew no bounds for
all, and on the white marble cross placed on his grave,
and "under a spray of his favourite passion-flower, were
the words of his choice, the story of his life—"

　　　　"Amavimus, amamus, amabimus,"

and above them circling round the cross—

　　　　"God is Love."

Such was Kingsley's life in Eversley from first to
last.　It was in complete harmony with the noble
chivalry and the high aims breathing in his writings
and social aims, extending wide and far his influences
beyond it.　It is a remarkable proof of the unity of
his life and mind, his simple activity in a small sphere
entirely corresponding with the creations of his genius
penetrating the wider world beyond.

CHAPTER III.

THE SAINT'S TRAGEDY—A POET'S SOCIAL AIMS.

"THE Abbey is open for the Canon and the Poet," wrote Dean Stanley to Mrs. Kingsley immediately after the death of her husband, and no one would have grudged him a place in Poets' Corner at that time, or now. Still, it is not on his poetry—*i. e.* in the restricted sense, to the exclusion of poetic fiction—that his fame must permanently rest. In ballad poetry among moderns Kingsley has not his equal, and his songs and some of his shorter pieces are exquisite. Moreover, all his prose writings, especially his novels, were interpenetrated with the spirit of poetry, and it may be added, without taking upon ourselves in this place to speak of Kingsley as the man of letters, had he devoted himself entirely to poetry and the drama, his emotional force, his undoubted power of description, his spiritual insight which enabled him to read nature like an "illuminated missal," the characters of which he understood sufficiently, as he puts it, so as to represent the unseen by the seen, and his aptness to throw a poetic charm around the most commonplace situations and events,

his love for the romantic, and above all his idealism—
all these were calculated to make of him a great poet.
But here we are only concerned to speak of his poetry
as interpreting his social aims and subjective experiences
in his social studies; as when in 1841 he tells us how—

> "Through sunless cities, and the weary haunts
> Of smoke-grimed labour, and foul revelry,
> My flagging wing has swept."

Why he flagged so soon after producing seven years later
the *Saint's Tragedy,* he has told us in one of his letters :

> "I never wrote five hundred lines in my life before the
> *Saint's Tragedy* . . . and I have not read half enough.
> I have been studying all physical sciences which deal with
> phenomena.   I have been watching nature in every mood :
> I have been poring over sculptures and paintings since I
> was a little boy—and all I can say is, I do not know half
> enough to be a poet in the nineteenth century, and have
> cut the Muse *pro tempore.*"

This was in December 1848, after the appearance of
his *chef d'œuvre,* his first and last attempt as far as we
know at dramatic writing.   It was the product of his
youthful mind, written under the pressure of social
and religious problems which then occupied him and
all the world, and bearing the unmistakable impress
of an overpowering intensity.   Hence it is not in
manner, polish of style, and artistic skill, all that
might be desired.   Though received with favour at
Oxford, Professor Conington wrote an unfavourable
review of it, which, however, led to a lifelong friend-
ship between author and critic—a professor of Greek
comparing it with classic models could not fail finding

fault with its incoherencies. The *Saint's Tragedy* comes nearer in its forcefulness and wealth of diction to the Elizabethan drama, though it could not bear a close comparison with Shakespere in his maturer productions, and Chevalier Bunsen's prediction that Kingsley was destined to carry on Shakespere's historical plays has not been fulfilled. The *Saint's Tragedy* bears traces of the restlessness of the nineteenth century, and Kingsley's own state of mental excitement; it lacks the quality of calm development and severe solemnity in the progress of its action which we look for in the most finished works of the tragedian. As in the poem on *The Bad Squire*, and *A New Forest Battle*, only preceding the *Saint's Tragedy* by a year, and some other poems in *Yeast* of the same period, there is too much visible effort, the fever-heat of the social passion is not only expanding the poet's soul, but detrimental to calm workmanship, cool self-recollection, and plastic force under control.

But there is the passionate glow in the poet's soul which richly compensates for the absence of these formative powers, and if we miss perfection of form, we are reconciled by the thought that there is here a perfect freedom from that artificiality and close attention to purity of style which, as in the case of the French tragedians, produces a sense of unreality and ineffectiveness. Kingsley was not the man to " behowl the moon in any poetry, however exquisite." We have here the poet at work, as described by himself, a

"Joyous knight-errant of God, thirsting for labour and strife," throwing himself heart and soul into his subject, seeing in St. Elizabeth a kindred spirit haunted by the thoughts and struggling with the problems which agitated his own soul, though how far and to what extent in his then disturbed state of mind he could not clearly determine. In one thing the aims were identical, to quote the last line in the poem addressed to the authoress of *Our Village,* in whom, too, he saw a kindred aim—

"To knit in loving knowledge rich and poor."

In the mediæval saint he saw the qualities of "wisdom, self-sacrifice, daring, and love" imperfectly displayed, which he knew were needed in all their plenitude for such a task. Love for the people was *the* link which most strongly attached the poet to the chief person in his creation. In this respect the *Saint's Tragedy* differs from the dramas of Shakespere and Goethe, in which "the people" do not form a conspicuous element, or where, at least, popular aspirations are not treated so seriously or sympathetically. In the *Tempest* the communistic ideal is held up to gentle ridicule. In the Roman and one or two English historical plays of Shakespere, popular leaders and those they lead receive scant consideration. We might quote a number of passages from *Faust* to illustrate Goethe's serene contempt for the social aspirations generally associated with the French Revolution. Love for the people, the democratic element in poetry, is of later growth. Even Tennyson's social philosophy has been characterized as anti-popular in this sense, the Poet Laureate himself as a "conservative believer in progress," and an "un-reforming optimist," rather than as an advocate of those who spend their life in laborious poverty and a prophet of social reform.[1] This was in 1874. Lord Tennyson has since become less a believer in progress, but not more a believer in popular movements and the power of the people to work out their own destiny. Kingsley in the *Saint's Tragedy* has nothing in his composition of the " Poet—Pangloss." He indeed knew the faults of the people, but never treats them with contemptuous pity. Yet his hand turns more readily to their would-be deliverer, St. Elizabeth, "the only healthy popish saint" in the Calendar.

As far back as 1843 the study of her life had occupied Kingsley's mind. Unlike the Comte de Montalembert, he has not told us how first he became acquainted with it. But as he shared some of the characteristics of the French nobleman—his impetuosity, his chivalry, and his manly love of fighting on the losing side for " God and Society," his immovable cloudless faith, his belief in the Church to become a "league for social good"; so, too, it may be surmised that in both cases it was elective affinity which drew both men to the same character in similar states of mind.

Similar but not identical feelings attracted the mind of Kingsley towards the Hungarian princess. To Kingsley the character of " Dear Elizabeth " has a

[1] See an article on Mr. Tennyson's "Social Philosophy," by Lionel Tollemache, in the *Fortnightly Review* for February 1874.

peculiar fascination, and in 1846, "Dear Elizabeth is now becoming too far developed to cut her in pieces, and serve her up in a magazine: she shall appear in a poem, if I wait seven years to finish her." But behold, in another year this resolution to follow the Horatian maxim is broken. After consulting with some of his friends, and encouraged by them to publish, especially by Maurice, who undertakes to submit the MS. to Mr. W. Coleridge, Tennyson, and "Van Artevelde Taylor," he hands it over to Parker, and writes to his friend Powles: "*St. Elizabeth* is in the press, having been taken off my hands by the heroic magnanimity of Mr. John Parker . . . no one else would have it."

A version of the story of Elizabeth in a dainty poetic form, peculiar to himself, has been lately given by Lewis Morris in his *Vision of Saints*, including many of the apocryphal incidents of her life omitted by Charles Kingsley, and we scarcely need dwell on these by way of introduction—how the young princess, living as a child and maiden in the uncongenial atmosphere of the Thuringian court as the affianced bride and wife of the young Landgrave Lewis, becomes a rare example of humble piety; how in her "great pity for the labouring world" she strips herself of gorgeous apparel to clothe the naked, and is reduced to beggary in feeding the hungry; how she empties the royal granaries to save the starving multitude, and when expelled the castle by court intrigues in the absence of her husband, she, even in a life of privation at Marburg, continues her

work of charity; how at last, and by order of her
relentless father confessor, the last luxury of giving is
withdrawn, and under a "soul-crushing asceticism" and
severe discipline her feeble frame gives way, and she
dies at the age of twenty-four, reverenced as a martyred
saint by those who, in her lifetime, added to the weight
of cares by their want of appreciating her single-minded
devotedness to duty. Mr. Maurice in the preface to the
Tragedy, and Kingsley in his own introduction to it,
have given us clearly to understand that the subjective
struggles of the heroine are intended to symbolize the
mental struggles of her age, the conflict between the
manly or human, and monkish or ecclesiastical ideal of
perfection, and also that the Tragedy is intended for the
study of those who watch or engage in the struggles of
soul peculiar to our own times, that here we have
reflected, in a picture of thirteenth-century life, the
spiritual conflicts of eager and earnest souls in the
nineteenth. Accordingly, we find in the first two Acts,
the theme is discussed how far marital love and the
possession of goods may be lawful and expedient for
those who would live the religious life; whether in an
age of "heathenry," where people swear " by the sleeve
of beauty, Madam," it is not the duty of the religious
to stem the tide of secularism by a complete abstraction
from the world : therefore, says Elizabeth—

"I'd die a saint !
Win heaven for her by prayers, and build great minster
    chantries and hospitals for her ; wipe out
By mighty deeds our race's guilt and shame."

Lewis, her affianced husband, almost anticipating Rousseau's revolt against the positive laws of property in civilized society, speaks of it thus :

> "Possession's naught ;
> A parchment ghost ; a word I am ashamed
> To claim even here, lest all the forest spirits,
> And bees who drain unasked the free-born flowers,
> Should mock, and cry, ' Vain man, not theirs, but ours.' "

When Walter of Varila, the incarnation of "healthy animalism," points out that "possession's beef and ale " —and moreover "the easiest trade of all, too "—Lewis inquires—

> "How now ?   What need then of long discipline,
> Not to mere feats of arms, but feats of soul,
> To courtesies and high self-sacrifice,
> To order and obedience, and the grace
> Which makes commands, requests, and service, favour.
> .   .   .   .
> Why then, if I but need, like stalled ox,
> To chew the grass cut for me."

Walter has his worldly-wise answer ready for him—

> "Custom and selfishness will keep all steady
> For half a life."

So speaks the "dawning manhood of Europe " in the thirteenth century, struggling to be free from the restraints of Christian ethics.   Of course the high-flown sentimentality of Lewis and Elizabeth meet with little favour in the world around them.   To it Elizabeth is only "a canting baby," who was christened a " brown mouse for her stillness," Lewis a besotted fool with his conscientious scruples.   Yet, fool as he is, he wisely discerns the unwisdom in the two extremes of Walter the Worldling and Conrad the Churchman. He reminds the former of the duties of property—" Toil is the true knight's portion"; he tells the latter that labour without love and the service of humanity without chivalric sentiment are incomplete. The worship of the Virgin, he shows, is not inconsistent with woman worship; as for himself, he prefers a living saint who can incite him to noble acts.

> " From her lips
> To learn my daily task ;—in her pure eyes
> To see the living type of those heaven-glories
> I dare not look on ;—let her work her will
> Of love and wisdom as these straining hinds ;—
> To squire a saint around her labour field,
> And she and it both mine ;—that was possession."

That living saint is Elizabeth, only she is too high above him in her exalted sense of duty, yet he reasons—

> " Is wedlock treason to that purity
> Which is the jewel and the soul of wedlock ?
> Elizabeth ! my saint !"

"You love her, then ?" inquires the shrewd Walter, who sees a healing quality in this mundane love for the " male hysterics" of impractical idealism and emasculating pietism. In answer to this a passage follows as near akin to Shakspere's playful muse as is to be met anywhere in its expression of youthful fondness. Elizabeth's struggle consists in this, that she has neither the stuff to be a nun right out, or to be a complete wife either, as she says herself—

> " Too weak to face the world, too weak to leave it."

But she is a woman, and all things bid her love. She, not being mistress of herself, sends for Lewis, accordingly,—"bring him to me—he is mine." And thus human love triumphs. After that doubt and self-distrust return with renewed force. " Have I two husbands ? " Can she be at the same time the spouse of Lewis and Heaven ? Taming "the rebel flesh " is hard. In her religious struggles she seeks refuge in a " boiling crater field of labour," healing the sick and soothing the sad. Thus, then, " two weakling children " err in their earnest search for the true path of duty. Thus the revelation comes to Elizabeth of the fearful state of things in the condition of those below her.

> " We sit in a cloud and sing like pictured angels,
> And say, the world runs smooth—while right below
> Welters the black fermenting heap of life
> On which our state is built."

She experiences what so many experience in the present day, resolves what some few high-souled men high-placed socially or intellectually above the crowd have attempted in their yearning to help the poor in their struggles—to mention a modern instance, Laurence Oliphant, to show that this species of mystic is not yet extinct—

> " I will taste somewhat this same poverty,
> Try these temptations, grudges, gnawing shames,
> For which 'tis blamed : how probe her unfelt ill ?
> Would'st be the poor man's friend ? Must freeze with him—
> Test sleepless hunger—let thy crippled back
> Ache o'er the endless furrow ; how was He,
> The blessed One, made perfect ? Why, by grief—

He read the tear-stained book of poor men's souls,
As I must learn to read it."

And so far from repenting of this act of self-effacement, forgets the whirl of doubt in happy toil, and exhorts others to find consolation in such holy effort.

" Be earnest, earnest, earnest ; mad, if thou wilt :
Do what thou dost as if the stake were heaven,
And that thy last deed ere the judgment day.
When all's done, nothing's done. There's rest above—
Below let work be death, if work be love ! "

In contrast with this there follows a scene in which nobles and Church dignitaries discuss economic questions quite in the orthodox fashion of the students of political economy in Kingsley's time. They talk fiercely of " the stern benevolence of Providence," teaching the poor " the need of self-exertion," and in the course of the conversation Conrad's sermon is mentioned in which he speaks of clerics " aping the artless cant of an aristocracy who made them, use them, and despise them"— was Kingsley acquainted with any such, we wonder, in his own day ?—and Count Walter breaks out in bitter persiflage against the small pedant,—" your closet philosopher, who has just courage enough to bestride his theory . . . for truly man was made for theories, not theories for man. A doctrine is then men's God—touch but that shrine, and lo ! your simpering philanthropist becomes a ruthless Dominican."

But the upshot of it all is, that Elizabeth follows her inner promptings during the short spell of happy married life, until Lewis follows *his* call, and goes forth

F

as a Crusader. In the severe trial of parting Elizabeth nearly gives way to feminine weakness, all but gratifying her enemy's sneer—

> "Those saints who fain would 'wean themselves from earth,'
> Still yield to the affections they despise
> When the game's earnest."

But then she recovers her power of resolve after a temporary yielding to human infirmity, and says—

> "Life is too short for mean anxieties:
> Soul, thou must work, though blindfold."

The next two Acts of the tragedy are full of her personal trials and wrongs endured heroically on the removal of her natural protector; she experiences, too, what few escape who come in close contact with the crowd, specially those who fall from high estate, however undeserved the fall may be—the ingratitude of the ignorant and the coarse unfeelingness of the ignoble. But perfected through suffering, she attains at last to "the strength which comes by suffering." She is far from being crushed by the failure of her self-imposed mission. For as her waiting-woman says—

> "These higher spirits must not bend
> To common methods; in their inner world
> They move by broader laws."

When the old nurse in the chamber of the Wartburg remonstrates with her for taking all this trouble "about the ungracious poor," Elizabeth only speaks of the duty of fasting and mourning while the bridegroom is away. When the new Landgrave's man sent to turn her out becomes rude with the coarseness of his kind,

she reasons sweetly with him, reminding him how she
nursed his wife in sickness, and when he proves imper-
vious to this argument, she still persists in trusting to
the higher instincts of the people—

> " Lead on : a people's love
> Shall right me."

When the monks refuse reluctantly to give her shelter
on the ground that they must obey the powers that be,
and Guta, her waiting-woman, exclaims—

> " Mean-spirited !
> Fair frocks hide foul hearts.   Why, their altar now
> Is blazing with your gifts "—

Elizabeth gently retorts—

> " Well—here's one lesson learned ! I thank thee, Lord !
> Henceforth I'll straight to Thee, and *to Thy poor*."

When an unworthy object of her bounty in better
days reads her a rasping lecture on her false humility
and "selfish hypocritic pride," using the poor man's
body as "stones to build withal your Jacob's ladder,"
to raise herself in the Scala Dei, Elizabeth accepts it as
a heaven-sent lesson, and even discerns much wisdom
in the crone's rebuke.

> " Dull boors
> See deeper than we think, and hide within
> Their leathern hulls unfathomable truths,
> Which we amid thought's glittering mazes lose.
> They grind among the iron facts of life,
> And have no time for self-deception."

Then again, by way of contrast, there follows an
exquisite bit of dialogue between Elizabeth and her

uncle the Bishop of Bamberg—a kind of Bishop Blou-
gram, the very picture of a mediæval Gallio, whose
great motto is, "We must be moderate : I hate over-
doing anything—especially religion," and he certainly
never errs in excess of religious zeal except in sanction-
ing the persecution of heretics. He serves as a foil
to bring out the ardour of his niece, whom an adverse
world has not been able to subdue, and who has been
taught a noble self-reliance by misfortune ; henceforth
she is independent of the world's praise and blame in
following her own ideal—

> "I have snapt opinion's chains, and now I'll soar
> Up to the blazing sunlight, and be free."

And so she leaves her uncle's palace for a hut or
cottage in Marburg. Here the climax of the struggle
is reached. She is taught to give up all, even her
children, though not without agonizing thought full of
doubt and despair accompanying the act of self-renunci-
ation. Here we hear the voice of the world's sorrow
muffled by mediæval surroundings, but, like the cry of
the human heart in all ages, as in Job, in the Prometheus,
in the Divine Comedy, in Hamlet, in Faust, so here in
St. Elizabeth it ends with a tone of sad resignedness,
in which we read something like the neo-stoicism of
our age, the Christian Iphigeneia self-immolated on
the Marburg high altar—

> "Come, the victim's ready."

Kingsley's power of entering into the mediæval spirit,
and speaking through Conrad the " heretic-catcher,"

from whom not only several centuries of thought, but
an impassable gulf of diversity of temperament separates
him, in his own thought more than once displays a gift
of spiritual assimilation rarely met even in kindred
minds. But here, as in the poem of St. Maura, we
have the same sympathetic appreciation of saintly
asceticism and pious mysticism which in turns attract
and repel his ardent spirit. "Even self-torture," he
remarks in the notes to the *Saint's Tragedy*, "will have
charms after the utter dryness and life-in-death of mere
ecclesiastical pedantry." But his inmost thoughts were
put into the lips of Walter of Varila, when he accuses
monkish piety, or rather charity, as "double-distilled
selfishness," which gives a "halfpenny for every halfpenny worth of eternal life"—"a private workshop in
which to work out her own salvation." What the
Catholic layman says of the merit-seeking saint in the
thirteenth has a meaning for the "piety pays best"
style of travestied Christianity held up to scorn by
Charles Kingsley in the nineteenth century—"I have
watched you and your crew, how you preach up selfish
ambition for Divine charity." Still Kingsley can see
deeper than this. He knows that the stuff of which
martyrs and mystics are made is finer by far than the
coarse clay which is moulded into our matter-of-fact
practical man of the world; that those who follow
Christ's law and example of self-extinction and self-
effacement find true happiness in altruistic endeavour,
though without seeking it. Quoth Elizabeth :

> "Ay, there lies the secret—
> Could we but crush that ever-craving lust
> For bliss, which kills all bliss, and lose our life,
> Our barren unit life, to find again
> A thousand lives in those for whom we die."

.   .   .   .   .

>   " Is selfishness
> For time a sin—spun out to eternity
> Celestial prudence ? Shame ! oh, thrust me forth,—
> Forth, Lord, from self, until I toil and die
> No more for heaven and bliss, but duty, Lord,
> Duty to Thee, although my meed should be
> The hell which I deserve ! "

Thus we find Elizabeth canonized not only in the Marburg convent, but in the literature of England, and at the very period when religious conventionality reigns supreme, when many there were ready to say with the monk in this tragedy, dwelling on the futility of social and religious reform, and the efforts of the "reformation bitten" Christian philanthropist : "Behold the fruit of your reformers ! This comes of their realized ideals, and centralizations, and organizations," &c., &c. Even the character of Conrad, whose narrow creed and cruel spirit of religious domination repels, assumes a nobler aspect towards the close ; the tragic horror inspired by his deeds and sufferings, in the end is softened into pity as we listen to the eager self-questionings of his perturbed soul, and the humble confession of his partial failure and mistakes made in good faith.

> "We make and moil, like children in their gardens,
>   And spoil with dabbled hands our flowers i' the planting,
>   And yet a saint is made."

.   .   .   .   .   .

> " And yet what matter ?
> Better that I, this paltry, sinful saint,
> Fall fighting, crushed into the nether pit,
> If my dead corpse may bridge the path to heaven,
> And damn itself, to save the souls of others."

He, too, has his terrible doubts of the efficacy of the religious system to which his life is consecrated ; but his powers are willingly sacrificed to it, and so he finds satisfaction in the one great work of his life, though, alas ! like all the rest, incomplete.

> " The work is done ! Diva Elizabeth !
> And I have trained one saint before I die ! "

And so he expires himself, a victim of his own immoderate zeal, unshaken to the last in his faith in God and the power of one saintly life, exclaiming—

> " O God ! a martyr's crown !   Elizabeth."

With these words concludes the *Saint's Tragedy.*

Elizabeth, this ethereal creature who will not wear a coronet in church, who prefers the cross to the crown,

> " Who shrines heaven's graces in earth's rich casket,"

who, in her sweet humility, shrinks from her high task in dread of the weakness of her own fine-wrought nature, and yet, " to find my strength in vastness," requiring a stronger will to lean against ; so fair in her innocent loveliness, that even the stern priests cannot help admiring it from a distance—

> " With such looks
> The Queen of heaven, perchance, slow pacing came
> Adown our sleeping wards, when Dominic
> Sank fainting, drunk with beauty ; she is most fair—"

so womanly in her affection for the husband, so devoted as a mother to the babes, while all the time more than half afraid of robbing heaven of its due of love and loyalty—is held up throughout as an example of conscientious performance of duty under difficulty, trying to reconcile the claims of personal and domestic duties with those appertaining to " God and society " and " God's poor."

Here, then, we have a drama and a tragedy, a picture of high life and low life with their limitations, in which the principal figure as well as the subordinate personages are very far from perfect, inconsistent with themselves, and often out of proper relation with the age in which they live ; out of place, so to speak, on the stage of life on which they appear. Thus Lewis wants the power of action in addition to his virtuous amiability and high notion of the sacredness of marriage. Conrad's noble character, with its depth of religious feeling and height of aspiration, lacking the breadth which prevents his becoming a really great reformer of his Church. The " noble lay-religion " of Walter is warped by a touch of scornful worldliness, and so—not to proceed any further into an analysis of less important personages—the drama becomes a tragedy. The actors being what they are, the whole must end in a catastrophe or failure. In this consists the tragic element.

We have been told that in this tragedy Kingsley sets up straw men to knock them down, that he keeps on thrashing a dead horse, or slaying the slain ; in short,

that the danger of asceticism gaining the upper hand in
England is an imaginary foe which it was not worth
while fighting. This may be true at this present
moment, though even now some forms of asceticism
have a charm for many minds, such as Pessimists with
Schopenhauer at their head, Theosophists, and modern
Buddhists, not to mention several varieties of Christian
ascetics in the Anglican and Roman Communion. In
1847, the danger, as it appeared to Kingsley's inflamed
brain, assumed more formidable proportions, and others,
more calm by disposition, shared with him both the
fear of Papal aggression and the revival of ascetic forms
of religion as represented by the Newmanites. Of these
were the late Prince Consort, a great admirer of the
Saint's Tragedy, and who, writing to his daughter in
Berlin in 1860, thus remarks on it—

" My best thanks for your kind letter of the twentieth of
June. I was certain that the *Saint's Tragedy* would not only
interest and impress you, but that you would comprehend
and grasp the inner spirit of the work. The substitution
of doctrines made by stupid men for laws of God-made
nature is the core of Catholicism—the good God did
not understand how to make His own world, nature is
wicked, given over to destruction—a thing to be abhorred.
Yet stay. Not so. The good God made it in the beginning
altogether good, and the devil has spoiled His handiwork ;
it is, to speak properly, the workmanship of the latter, and
God is unable to help Himself. Then comes the Church
and helps Him out of His trouble ; she destroys the
wicked, degenerate nature for Him, and magnanimously
gives Him His own.

" This is the true meaning of the flesh and the devil,

as presented by the Church. Kingsley has depicted this work of the Church in all its purity in ' Elizabeth the Saint,' and the reader's own nature shudders before the image of what the Church has substituted for God's own work." [1]

But we must also take into account another sense under the immediate influence of which the *Saint's Tragedy* was written—the public mind was so agitated by the " social condition of the people " question, and the attitude of the Church towards it. This gives it its social colouring, and when the time has come for the literary history of England in the nineteenth century to be written by a competent hand, the *Saint's Tragedy* will in it occupy an honoured place as a powerful dramatic expression of the social aspirations, from a religious point of view, in 1848, as conceived not too clearly, but entertained none the less fervently by one of the most generous spirits of that time.

In the same way perhaps Ibsen's social dramas will rank high as an expression of a similar feeling at a later period of the same eventful century, which still more than Kingsley's tragedy reflect the disheartening sense of futility in attempts of social amelioration and the struggles after a higher ideal against surrounding prejudice and passion, besotted ignorance, and irrational opposition to new ideas. We may be pardoned, therefore, if we add a few remarks by way of comparison and contrast between these two writers by way of concluding this chapter. Both the *Saint's Tragedy* and

[1] *The Life of the Prince Consort*, by Theodore Martin, vol. iv. p. 340.

most of Ibsen's plays have this in common—that they were not intended for actual representation on the stage, though Ibsen, having himself been royal stage-manager at one period of his life, has this advantage over Kingsley in knowing the possibilities and limitations of tragic effect, and the secrets of the art in bringing them about. Again, we have in both more or less burning questions of the day as affecting modern society and social morality discussed, though this is done directly by Ibsen, and only indirectly by Kingsley. In this discussion, however, there is a wide difference in the attitude of mind of the respective writers, separated as they are by nearly half a century of continually developed thought and discussion since the *Saint's Tragedy* was written. Ibsen is a realist, and writes with the "realistic temper"; Kingsley is an idealist, and writes under the full sway of the "idealistic fancy." True, there is much realism in his art, so much, indeed, that to some minds he has proved even offensive. Ibsen is an idealist in his own way. "Do not despise idealists," says one of the characters in *Ghosts*, "or they will avenge themselves." But a trenchant and severe criticism of our present society rather than the creation of ideal characters, such as St. Elizabeth, is the predominating trait of Ibsen's work.

Another coincidence in connection with this subject is the place assigned to woman in the regeneration of society; both Ibsen and Kingsley look to woman's influence as a means for the possible realization of a higher social ideal. Most of the women in Ibsen's dramas are better than the men; and the perfect woman, though very far from coming up to the standard of Elizabeth, appears on the stage as the saving power amid the deformities of social life. This comes out especially in *Pillars of Society*, where Lona reforms one of these "Pillars," who has well-nigh ruined the lives of three women, assisted by her younger brother, the supposed scapegrace, but who really becomes the scapegoat to redeem the really worthless character of Bernick. But the grand energy of the women in these plays does not compare with the manifold graces of Diva Elizabeth, nor the description given of woman's saving power in the "Triumph of Woman," sketched in *Yeast*.

Another coincidence we find in the common faith of both Kingsley and Ibsen in the effects of sanitary reform. In *An Enemy of Society* the principal character, Doctor Stockmann, is proved in the end to be after all "a true friend of the town; he is the saviour of society," in pointing out the dangerous condition of watering-places from a sanitary point of view. But he is overpowered by the selfish greed of his fellow-citizens, who would much rather the truth were suppressed, so as not to hinder a considerable influx of visitors; from which the man of science deduces a theory most pessimistic in its character. Not only are the water-works poisonous and the hygienic baths built on soil teeming with pestilence, but there is a further discovery, that " all our spiritual sources of life are poisoned, and that our whole

bourgeois society rests upon a soil teeming with the
pestilence of lies." Here we have none of the hopefulness of Kingsley on the same subject; and that the
author speaks here his own thoughts is evident from
the conclusion of the drama, where the hero of the play
says in view of the rottenness of society—" You see, the
fact is, that the strongest man upon earth is he who
stands most alone." The development of the individual seems to be Ibsen's ideal; it is Carlyle's one-man
theory. The man of iron will is wanted to save the
worldly crew we call Society, and woman's destiny it
is to help in forming strong characters. " All these
majority-truths are like last year's salt pork; they are
like rancid, mouldy ham, producing all the moral
scrofula that devastates society." Thus speak the men,
mostly like cynics and fatalists, whilst the women are
strong in character, standing by the few strong individual souls to support them in their manly struggles.
Such are Lona, Mrs. Alving, Petra, even in a way
Hetta. What is required, therefore, according to
Ibsen's social philosophy, is the creation of a masculine
aristocracy, an aristocracy of will, to make every man
in the land a *noble*man, and so counteract the morally
depressing influences of democratic institutions.

We have here some of the social theories of
Kingsley, too, but with a difference. Ibsen dwells
mainly on variation of type in his belief in the evolution of a higher morality, and only brings in the
principle of heredity in its power of transmitting evil
qualities. Kingsley, as a believer in fixity of form, is a

believer in hereditary powers and qualities, ancestral traits for good preserved as types of moral excellence, and therefore he writes in a letter to a friend—"A true democracy, such as you and I should wish to see, is impossible without a Church and a Queen, and, as I believe, without a gentry." [1] Moreover, he is a thorough believer in the gradual development of the aristocratic temper of mind, and with a chivalric love of the past combines a better hope for man generally in the social evolution of the future. He, too, sees like Ibsen much that raises anger and disgust in the social falsities of our modern life; but he does not think with the Danish dramatist the world is all built over with whited sepulchres. Ibsen is hopeless because uninspired by the religious faith which sustains Kingsley. Herein lies the essential discrepancy between the two writers, in whom all along we have traced so many striking resemblances. And yet such is the power of faith in the future, even in the most hopelessly desponding social pessimist, that even Bernick in the closing words of the play is made to say by way of giving effect to the author's theory, " It is you women who are the pillars of society." Lona replies, " No, no, the spirits of truth and freedom—these are the pillars of society." To this saying Kingsley could not have objected, though he probably would have added, " Where

---

[1] In one of the sermons on national subjects he points out that the true gentleman or lady are known by their unselfish love and devotion to the common weal, irrespective of birth and inherited status.

the Spirit of the Lord is, there is liberty," and again, "The truth shall make you free."

In short, Kingsley's social drama is religious not only in the choice of its subject, but in its conception and tendencies. To borrow the words of Maurice in the preface to it, where he expresses the confidence, " that the life of each man, and the life of this world, is a drama, in which a perfectly Good and True Being is unveiling His own purposes, and carrying on a conflict with evil, which must issue in complete victory." Religion after all is optimistic. Ibsen, in his power of dissecting in a merciless severity and unerring force of delineation the vices of society, being only a natural realist, keeps too close on the ordinary level of the stage of life ; we miss the lifting power supplied by religion of soaring above this " low-roofed life " of ours. Kingsley, without losing sight of the base facts of life and the hypocrisies in the social world, the brutality of personal egotism and the insufficiency in many respects of social institutions in counteracting these powers of evil, yet has sufficient faith in individual regeneration and social reform to place a figure on the stage which is the noble exhibition of self-sacrifice. She becomes an instrument of healing like the serpent raised in the wilderness, in conscious endeavour of imitating Him whose life and sufferings it was intended to prefigure. " Work and despair not " is its lesson. The individual, who is striving to rise above the dead level of ordinary ethics, individual or social, according to Ibsen, is in constant danger of being crushed by the all-powerful-ness of a faulty system of society. According to Kingsley, the personal excellences of individual character and the spiritual forces in society combined, mutually elevating, and conjointly developing under a Divine impulse, and constantly subjected to Divine direction, bring about a gradual transformation in the unit and the aggregate. The old Berseker spirit in both these modern men cries out, " Be strong." " Be strong in yourself," says Ibsen. " Be strong in the Lord, and the power of His might," says Kingsley. It is not hard to see which of the two has the most bracing effect on effort and endeavour in the moral and social elevation of mankind. In their differences of style and treatment arising from their different views of man in society, we note the impassable chasm which separates the mere social critic or modern social neologian from the Christian socialist—a chasm wide as the difference between hope and despair.

CHAPTER IV.

WHAT was said of the social drama in the last chapter applies with equal force to the social novel, *i. e.* the novel written with a purpose, either to describe the effects of certain social evils, or to propound given methods of dealing with social problems. It spoils the novel from the purely artistic point of view, and fails to produce the effect expected from it, in rousing a feeling of antagonism in the general reader, who resents being taken in by what pretends to be a story told for his amusement, but is really "a story with a meaning," a parable to convey dry lessons in political economy. Yet novelists of the day, such as *e. g.* Tourgenieff, in drawing vivid pictures of country life in Russia, calling the attention of the reader to the severe trials and troubles of the agricultural labourer, or Mr. Gissing, describing with earnestness and fervour the struggles of the "nether world" in English cities as "a protest against those brute forces of society which fill with wreck the abysses of the nether world," have been eminently successful in this modern department of

G

light literature. But this, we think, not so much because of the increased interest taken nowadays in social problems, though that counts for something, but because novel readers are so much captivated by the style of these proficients in story-telling that they resign themselves to being lectured on social subjects conveyed so pleasantly and without taxing too severely their attention. Thus, *Father and Sons*, or Mr. Baring Gould's *Arminel*, are devoured greedily by men or women who care little for Russian Mujics or plain English John Hodge.) But this cannot be said of the construction or contents of *Yeast*. It was written under pressure, and somewhat hurriedly. But then, it appeared at the right moment, and was the natural outcome of strong feeling in the author appealing to others who felt strongly in sympathy with him. Kingsley's mind as well as that of the country was in a state of seething, as the title of the novel suggests. To this must be attributed its success. It took up the agricultural labour question in a forcible way, and it occupied itself with another stirring question of the hour, the religious controversy in connection with *Tracts for the Times*. Moreover, appearing as it did in the form of a serial story in *Fraser*, it "took" the public from the first, and did not weary, as the economic and ecclesiastic controversies with which it is interlarded were administered in small doses, one at a time by way of monthly instalments, the intervals of suspense keeping up an interest in the course of the story. We are told that, written for the greater part at night when the day's work was over, it proved too much for brain and nerves, and that the author broke down at last from over-exertion, and that even temporary change and rest did not restore him entirely, and that he sunk again under it.   This accounts for some of its faults, which none knew better than Charles Kingsley.   Writing in 1848 to Professor Conington, and dwelling on its demerits, he expresses an intention of laying it aside *pro tem.*, to ferment for a few years ; but the fermentation, as far as we know, never led to anything like a thorough redaction ; there are at least no signs of mellow maturity.   It is as well, perhaps, that it should be so. For the chief merit of *Yeast* is its being written under the inspiration of the moment, and therefore presenting us with an exact portrait of the author's state of mind at the time, and an equally faithful picture of that of the public, both agitated and distracted, tossed about by the social cyclone then passing over the country.   Its vivid description of field sports proved so attractive to some readers, that officers in the army, returning from foreign service, would go straight to Eversley to see with their own eyes and hear with their own ears the parson who " could give such a picture of a hunting scene as the one in the opening chapter of *Yeast.*"   Moreover, the dwellers in cities, who were called upon in the then discontented state of the country districts to form an opinion on the Agrarian question, readily turned to these pleasant papers in a popular magazine, written by a man who professed to be and was something of a " practical agriculturist," and whom the peasants would listen to when he preached to them on such exciting subjects as poaching, emigration, and the rest of the burning questions of the hour.

We will now give a short analysis of the book, which will best indicate its character and tendencies. The hero is introduced in the hunting scene referred to above, with these two sides to his character, as dashing and devout, clever and melancholy, at the same time; " an unlicked bear, with sorrows before him." On riding dreamily after hounds he is arrested in the midst of solemn reflections, as unusual in the hunting field as a copy of the *Devout Life* of Francis of Sales, which by a mischance tumbles out of his pocket, by the sudden appearance of the heroine, "with her perfect masque, and queenly figure and earnest, upward gaze, who might have been the very model from which Raphael conceived his glorious Catharine." Her sudden apparition produces a mighty rush, followed by a fearful fall of the hero with momentous consequences, for the disabled huntsman is carried to her father's mansion to recover from the severe injuries received. Argemone is a fair specimen of the ritualistic devotee, and possesses in her character the elements of graceful asceticism and elegant mysticism. In a walk by moonlight with the hero, who by this time has sufficiently advanced in convalescence, she discovers that she is the destined instrument to bring about his conversion, and takes steps accordingly to bring it about. The interesting fox-hunter's stay is prolonged, and he makes

the acquaintance of Tregarva, "a stately, thoughtful-
looking Cornishman, some six feet three in height,
with thews and sinews in proportion," one of the
keepers, who throughout the book is the principal
spokesman of his class, from whom we learn the state
of the country, and who suggests the remedies to improve the condition of agricultural labour. All his
sayings might be prefaced with *loquitur* Charles
Kingsley. Take for example the following—

"Do you mean," says Lancelot (the hero of the story),
"that the unhealthiness of the country is chiefly caused by
the river?"

"No, sir," replies Tregarva, "the river damps are God's
sending; and so they are not too bad to bear."

"What do you mean?"

"Are men likely to be healthy when they are worse
housed than a pig?"

"No."

"And worse fed than a hound?"

"Good Heavens! No!"

"Or packed together to sleep like pilchards in a
barrel?"

"But, my good fellow, do you mean that the labourers
here are in that state?"

"It isn't far to walk, sir. Perhaps some day, when the
May-fly is gone off, and the fish won't rise awhile, you
could walk down and see. I beg your pardon, sir, though,
for thinking of such a thing. They are not places fit for
gentlemen, that's certain."

Here we hear, as it were, Kingsley discoursing on
health. Tregarva, in the course of the same conver-
ation, speaks of the parsons; and he does so very much
à la Kingsley—

"The parsons are afraid of the landlords. They must
see these things, for they are not blind; and they try to
plaster them up out of their own pockets. . . . And
as for the charitable great people, sir, when they see
poor folk sick or hungry before their eyes they pull out
their purses fast enough, God bless them!—for they
wouldn't like to be so themselves. But the oppression
that goes on all the year round; and the want that goes
on all the year round; and the filth, and the lying, and the
swearing, and the profligacy that go on all the year round;
and the sickening weight of debt, and the miserable grinding anxiety from rent-day to rent-day, and Saturday night
to Saturday night, that crushes a man's soul down, and
drives every thought out of his head but how he is to fill
his stomach, and warm his back, and keep a house over his
head, till he daren't for his life take his thoughts one
moment off the meat that perisheth—oh, sir, they never
felt this; and, therefore, they never dream that there are
thousands who feel this, and feel nothing else."

Tregarva is attracted towards and attracts in turn
the sister of Argemone, Honoria, which introduces
another element of the romantic to give additional
spice to the story, because of the disparity of station
in the principals of this story. As an instance, showing
how Kingsley manages to weave social theories into the
texture of his novel, the following passage may serve to
illustrate—

"Ask that sweet and heavenly angel, Miss Honoria,"—
and the keeper again blushed,—"and she, too, will tell you.
I think sometimes if she had been born and bred like her
father's tenants' daughters, to sleep where they sleep, to
hear the talk they hear, and see the things they see, what
would she have been now? We mustn't think of it." And

the keeper turned his head away, and fairly burst into tears.

At intervals, as we have hinted already, by way of interlude, or intermezzo, we are treated with bits of epistolary controversy carried on between Lancelot and his cousin Luke, a victim of Puseyism, which at this time was Kingsley's *bête noire*, and which he represents in its most unattractive features; even in his arguments on the subject with his lady-love he shies stones "at the rickety old windmill of sham-Popery which you have taken for a real giant." In opposing the mediæval idea of sanctity, as he does in the *Saint's Tragedy*, he almost approaches the Scylla of modern Philistinism in the attempt at escaping from the Charybdis of mystic pietism, as when in one of his letters to Luke he says—

"Give me the political economist, the sanitary reformer, the engineer ; and take your saints and virgins, relics and miracles.   The spinning-jenny and the railroad, Cunard's liners and electric telegraph, are to me, if not to you, signs that we are, on some points at least, in harmony with the universe ; that there is a mighty spirit working among us, who cannot be your anarchic and destroying devil, and therefore may be the Ordering and Creating God."

From such digressions into the field of theological controversy we are all the more ready to follow our author returning to discuss the main problem.   For this purpose he arranges a dinner-party.   Here we are invited to listen to a conversation on the condition of the agricultural labourer by representative persons

connected with the "landed interest." There is Lord
Minchampstead, at whose table they meet, a keen,
ready, and business-like strong man, the son of plain
Mr. Obadiah Newbroom, who had stood behind the
loom, but in course of time had developed into a manufacturer, and tells his son, "I have made a gentleman of
you; you must make a nobleman of yourself." The son
followed out his father's advice, and so becomes "the
owner of Minchampstead Park and 10,000 acres, for
two-thirds its real value, from that enthusiastic sportsman Lord Peu de Cervelle, whose family had come in
with the Conqueror, and gone out with George IV."
But though he had avowed at his own table soon after
he came into the country that " he had bought Minchampstead for merely commercial purposes, as a profitable investment of capital, and he would see that,
whatever else it did, it should *pay*," he was none the
less a fair and good-natured landlord, not forgetting his
duty to his tenantry and subordinates. Here, too, was
Colonel Bracebridge, the plucky sportsman, with better
ideals in his head than could appear from the record
of his life, a class of well-bred scapegrace for whom
Kingsley entertained a sneaking affection; it is he who
points to the clergy as the potential social reformers in
country districts: "They have the game in their own
hands, if they did but know how to play it." The host,
of course, takes a different view.

"All the modern schemes for their amelioration, which
ignore the laws of competition, must end either in pauper-
ization, or in the destruction of property."

Lord Vieuxbois represents the country magnate of the old school.

"Really I do not see," said Vieuxbois, "why people should wish to rise in life. They had no such self-willed fancy in the good old times. The whole notion is a product of these modern days."

Here our hero breaks in with Kingsley's own characteristic vehemence—

"I think honestly," said Lancelot, whose blood was up, "that we gentlemen all run into the same fallacy. We fancy ourselves the fixed and necessary element in society, to which all others are to accommodate themselves : ' Given the rights of the few rich, to find the condition of the many poor.' It seems to me that other postulate is quite as fair : ' Given the rights of the many poor, to find the condition of the few rich.' "

Lord Minchampstead laughed.

"If you hit us so hard, Mr. Smith, I must really denounce you as a communist. Lord Vieuxbois, shall we join the ladies?"

Thenceforward the hero begins in earnest the study of the problem, and this by means of personal observation. One of the subjects of social dissection is the poacher Crawey, of whom as well as his natural enemy Harry, the old-fashioned gamekeeper, we have a most powerful description; there are besides some thrilling scenes of poachers' frays full of *esprit* and instinct with passion, and all this to awaken interest in such lives as theirs, especially poor Crawey's; but the reader is more puzzled than ever with the problem before him. Is society answerable for the wrongs of law-breakers like

Crawey? is he past recovery? is he capable of higher things? who is at fault? has this man sinned or his betters in putting him where he is, and leaving him to the tender mercies of the Game Laws? The riddle is left unsolved, and poor Crawey unreclaimed. Argemone in the meantime has succeeded not in converting Lancelot, but in making him her slave. He avows his love in a sketch he draws of the " Triumph of Woman," which is an elaborate, perhaps too elaborate, piece of writing, and, like most of Kingsley's best bits, spoiled slightly by a tone of exaggeration; but as a confession of love it is, as may be expected, successful, and henceforth the ideas of social reformation are shared by the two lovers. The interest of the story turns on the question, who is to win the victory, the hero or the father-confessor of Argemone, *i.e.* her parish priest? where is her lot to be cast, in the world or in the church? will she embrace the spiritual life, or become the wife of Lancelot? The course of true love does not run smooth, and Tregarva gets into serious trouble. He has written a ballad on the Game Laws with a strong flavour of rural socialism; it falls into the hands of the Squire, who in his wrath dismisses him on the spot. A blow, too, is impending over the hero's head. His uncle's bank, where his whole fortune is invested, is on the point of stopping payment. The catastrophe might be averted by Argemone's spiritual director, the Vicar, who carries a letter from the banker to Lancelot, on the prompt delivery of which all depends. But in an evil hour the priest elects to delay it, knowing full well that this involves the ruin of Lancelot, and so would put an end to the plan of his union with Argemone. The letter is not delivered in time, and the crash comes. Here is a fair opportunity for attacking our modern credit system, and the author avails himself of it promptly enough, showing at the same time the inconsistency of modern religious profession, and modern methods of money-making.

"If I were a Christian," said Lancelot, "like you, I would call this credit system of yours the devil's selfish counterfeit of God's order of mutual love and trust; the child of that miserable dream which, as Dr. Chalmers well said, expects universal selfishness to do the work of universal love. . . ." "Selfishness can collect, not unite, a herd of cowardly wild cattle that they may feed together, breed together, keep off the wolf and bear together. But when one of your wild cattle falls sick, what becomes of the corporate feeling of the herd then? For one man of your class who is nobly helped by his fellows, are not the thousand left behind to perish? Your Bible talks of society, not as a herd, but as a living tree, an organic, individual body, a holy brotherhood, and Kingdom of God. And here is an idol which you have set up instead of it."

In this complicated state of affairs, a *Deus ex machinâ* is brought on the scene in the next chapter, but without satisfactorily clearing up the difficulties of the plot, and so to the last we are left to a great extent mystified as to the final issue. This strange person, Barnakill by name, who also severely inveighs against capitalism in its alliance with modern Pharisaism, is not very successful in his attempt to throw a "supra-lunar illumination on social questions"; there is but a very dim light thrown by him on the leaden sky of economic disquisition. There is little interest in the rest of the story except its tragical close. The heroine dies of a fever caught in visiting some of her father's cottages; it is the Nemesis avenging culpable neglect of sanitary precautions. Her sister, too, falls a victim to disease, the curse of the Lavingtons which has come upon them both. But Argemone in her dying words bids Lancelot to labour on in the cause of the poor. What he actually performs under such an inspiration we are not told. *Omnia exeunt in mysterium*, that is the phrase which Charles Kingsley quotes in the Epilogue by way of excuse for such a mystified ending. Goethe, too, referring to the mystical close of the second Faust, once remarked, in "old age we all turn mystics." But then Kingsley could not plead old age when he concluded his story, and Lancelot is not like Faust, the author's own portrait, although *Yeast* was from the first, like Faust, to be mythical and typical. Kingsley also anticipates adverse criticism on the fragmentary character of the book as a whole, without making out a good case for himself. But what is the most melancholy part of the book, is the desponding tone in which it speaks of possible future reforms—

"For the present, the poor of Whitford, owing, as it seems to them and me, to quite other causes than an 'over-stocked labour-market,' or 'too rapid multiplication of the species,' are growing more profligate, reckless, pauperized, year by year.

"I have set forth, as far as in me lay, the data of the problem ; and surely if the premises be given, wise men will not have to look far for the conclusion. In homely English I have given my readers *Yeast ;* if they be what I take them for, they will be able to bake with it themselves."

We may inquire how far are the data supported by the sober statements of others, and what is pure fancy and fiction ? and again, what success have the bakers with such yeast attained to thus far in producing bread and not a stone for those who ask for it ?   Some of the data are referred to by the author of *Perils of the Nation,* a work which Kingsley had studied with deep interest. He quotes p. xxv from Mr. Twistleton's report on the "Sanitary Inquiry," where we are told that owing to the paucity of small farms the English agricultural labourer has not the slightest prospect of rising in the world and becoming a small farmer himself except by emigration. Again, on pp. 77, 78, speaking of the enormous accumulations of property in one hand, he points out the dangerous power thus placed in that hand over labourers depending entirely on their weekly wages and the roof over their head on the large landed proprietor who employs them.   Living as they do "in hovels, singly or clustered, destitute of comfort, cramping the body, and depressing the mind," . . . ": they follow the lowest instincts and impulses of animal life, and are perfectly prepared to become the scourges of those orders of society who have trampled them down to so wretched a level."   If we compare this with what the author of *Yeast* says in the chapter entitled "A Village Revel," giving what might seem a too dreary description of the daily life of English rustics, we may see how sadly true to life it was then, how sadly true to life it is but in too many instances even now; "they are a stupid, pig-headed generation at the best." Lancelot had expected at the end "to hear something of pastoral sentiment, and of genial, frolicsome humour; to see some innocent, simple enjoyment; but instead, what had he seen but vanity, jealousy, hoggish sensuality, dull vacuity—drudges struggling for one night to forget their drudgery. And yet, withal, their songs and the effect which they produced showed that in these poor creatures, too, lay the germs of pathos, taste, melody, soft and noble affections."

And what can you expect from men in their hopeless state? "Day-labourer born, day-labourer live, from hand to mouth, scraping and grinding to get not meat and beer even, but bread and potatoes; and then, at the end of it all, for a worthy reward, half-a-crown a week of parish pay—or the workhouse. That's a lively, hopeful prospect for a Christian man." What does such a one say but *Nihil habeo, nihil curo.* "What makes me maddest of all, sir," says Tregarva, "is to see that everybody sees these evils except just the men who can cure them—the squires and the parsons." True, they are ready enough with patronizing charities. There is Lord Vieuxbois spending his whole life and time among the poor; "he fats prize labourers, sir, just as Lord Minchampstead fats prize oxen and pigs."

What Kingsley says of the pressure of the system in

degrading the women and driving the men to despair,
and depopulating the country districts, leaving a resi-
duum sunk to the lowest depth, and a race of children
growing up over-educated and under-fed; of the waste
of human life, in fact waste of everything; "waste of
manure, waste of land, waste of muscle, waste of brain,
waste of population—and we call ourselves the workshop
of the world!"—all this is fully corroborated by the statements drawn from official reports and writers of the time
speaking with authority, and receive further illustration
from the letters of S. G. O., Kingsley's brother-in-law
and brother-in-arms, fighting against the same enemy—
agricultural distress, physical, moral, and spiritual.

What Kingsley suggested by way of solving it must
be gathered from hints in *Yeast*, and a published lecture
on "the application of associative principles and methods
to agriculture," in which he addresses himself to the
task in an unwonted spirit of calm deliberation, and
also some few allusions to the subject scattered over
the two volumes of Memories of his life. But before
we proceed to compare his proposals with those of some
others, we would in this place compare the manner in
which the general question is treated in *Yeast* and
Coningsby, as these two novels may be said to represent the rival theories on the agricultural question of
the two Young England parties of that day, the reactionary *jeunesse dorée*, led by Lord Beaconsfield, and the
party, if we may so call it, of Religious Radicalism led
by Charles Kingsley and his master, F. D. Maurice, as
far as the latter permitted himself to be forced into

such a prominent position of leadership. The Tories
agreed with the Christian Socialists in this, that the
squires and the clergy were the men to cure the evils
complained of. " Property is the natural protector of
labour," said the former, but replies Kingsley in *Yeast*,
" I question whether it will suit the people themselves,
unless they can make property understand that it owes
them something more definite than protection." And
it is in this that the two novels differ most radically in
both their principles and proposals. The author of
Coningsby is more skilful as a novelist, if not in the
inventiveness of plot—both novels are poor in this
respect—at least in the literary art of interesting presentment and exquisite workmanship. He also excels
the author of *Yeast* in the grasp of political questions,
and his experience in the practical working of social
politics. This, however, suggests one of its principal
faults ; all is made to subserve his political party ends,
whereas *Yeast* has the advantage of being a work evidently coming from the heart, and in its absorbing
earnestness and unadulterated enthusiasms appealing
to the generous youth of England. In working out its
social problems, or rather in putting the problem before
the reader with perfect frankness and high-toned moral
and religious fervour, it touches a sympathetic chord in
the more emotional, and carries conviction to the more
rational inquirers into the great questions of the day.
The Church, to Mr. Disraeli, is an institution among
others important in the national life, and helping in
shaping the destiny of the people. He is, above all

things, a politician, and as such he speaks of the clergy
in *Coningsby* in this fashion, " The priests of God are
the tribunes of the people "—though he adds, in a tone
almost the same as that we note in *Yeast*, " O,
ignorant! that with such a mission they should ever
have cringed in the antechambers of ministers, or bowed
before parliamentary committees." But he is very far
from attaching the *spiritual* importance to the moral
and religious force exercised by " the priests of the
Lord " in the emergency of great social movements,
like Kingsley, who, referring to the democratic element
in Christ, and the mistaken notion of the Chartists
about the Church being an outworn aristocratic institution, writes to Ludlow in 1850—" If the priests of
the Lord are wanting to the cause now, woe to us! "
Both denounce with equally trenchant severity the
utilitarian selfishness of the age. " Life is much
easier," said Lord Everingham. " Life easy! " said
Lord Henry Sydney; " life appears to me to be a
fierce struggle." " Manners are easy," said Coningsby;
" and life is hard." " And I wish things exactly the
reverse," said Lord Henry. " The means and modes of
subsistence less difficult ; the conduct of life more
ceremonious." " Civilization has no time for ceremony,"
said Lord Everingham. This may be called the
Romanticist aspect of the question. It is the cry of
Wordsworth in his sonnet on Milton—

> " We are selfish men.
> Oh, raise us up, return to us again ;
> And give us manners, virtue, freedom, power."

H

* Or that of another sonnet of the same year, 1802—

> " Rapine, avarice, expense,
> This is idolatry ; and these we adore :
> Plain living and high thinking are no more :
> The homely beauty of the good old cause
> Is gone ; our peace, our fearful innocence,
> And pure religion, breathing household laws."

Kingsley goes further into the marrow of the matter in pointing out the rottenness of the selfish basis of society. Both attribute the evils complained of to the industrial revolution commencing when Wordsworth thus wrote, "the hurry-scurry of money-making, men-making, machine-making," which put the social organism out of joint, and the consequent clamour of suffering labour in what Kingsley calls the spirit of these rattling railway days; it brought in a new social force, the "social power" of Demos, seeking, as Coningsby says, "a specific for the evils of our social system in the general suffrage of the population."

But whereas the restoration of "the ancient order of the peasantry" to its pristine condition is the one thing needed, according to the chief speaker in *Coningsby*, Kingsley points to education, sanitary reform, and the raising of the status in the agricultural population in keeping with modern requirements and aspirations growing out of modern ideas. "Let me see property acknowledging, as in the old time of faith, that labour is its twin-brother, and that the essence of all tenure is the performance of duty," says Coningsby. That duty consists in paying better wages, giving better homes, and holding out better prospects of rising in the social scale, is the answer to this given in *Yeast*.   In *Coningsby* it is the rich manufacturer, the enemy of an hereditary aristocracy, and an abettor of democratic Radicalism as a means to crush the latter, who has the moral and physical well-being of the people at heart, building homes and cottages on a new system of ventilation, allotted gardens, and the rest, not an aristocratic landlord like the Duke.   This is significant.   Lord Minchampstead is represented in the same way, but to show that he follows the aristocratic tendencies of the ancient order of landed proprietors.   Here the authors of *Yeast* and *Coningsby* change sides, and for this reason.   The latter wants to stimulate his own party of squirearchy to emulate the Plutocracy in popular social reforms which shall preserve the order; the former sets forth the importance of creating, not only preserving, the aristocratic element in a new society, to give a new meaning to *noblesse oblige* in an age given to ignoble money-grubbing and self-seeking, and finding, so to speak, a middle course between feudal ties which are of the past and money ones which are of the present; in looking to the new proprietors gradually superseding the old, traders become rich and ennobled, buying up estates here, there, and everywhere, displacing the ancient nobility; and, as he says in another place, entering "into a true chivalrous competition against the ancestral owners of the neighbouring estates, to see if he cannot surpass them . . . an excellent landlord, presenting to me one of the most pleasant spectacles on English soil

at this day." But, again, the position of the two representatives of the old order and the new, respectively,
are the reverse of what we should expect them to be
when Disraeli speaks in glowing terms of Manchester
as the "metropolis of labour," and goes on magnilo-
quently after his fashion to say that, rightly understood,
"Manchester is as great a human exploit as Athens.
. . . It is the philosopher alone who can conceive the
grandeur of Manchester, and the immensity of its
future." "The earth hath bubbles, and such cities as
Manchester are of them," says Kingsley. The reason
of this divergence is that love of a "splendid materiality,"
of which the mind of Disraeli with its Semitic bent
could not divest itself to the last, for *Endymion* is full
of it, whilst that of Kingsley, full of that spirituality
which his purely Arian mind imbibed from Plato,
is after all antagonistic to the trading class, though it
produces its princely merchants vying in princely muni-
ficence with landed magnates who lack the money which
can alone purchase magnificence in these degenerate days.
They are necessary, he would say, for the present distress;
they and their capital help to bridge over the transition
from the old social order of the past to the new social
order of rural industry in the future.

Both authors are in perfect agreement on one point,
that the attempt to reconstruct society in its present
state of disorganization "on a purely rational basis,"
as Sidonia calls it, is a mistake. "There has been an
attempt to reconstruct society on a basis of material
motives and calculations. It has failed," he says. Of

course, this is an attack against individualism from the Conservative point of view, to hint at the disintegrating effects of weakening the authority of custom and long-established institutions. Kingsley, on the other hand, directs his attack against individualism in its economic rather than its political aspect, and tries to show in *Yeast* how God has set His seal on "a state of society which confesses its economic relations to be so utterly rotten and confused that it actually cannot afford to save yearly millions of pounds' worth of the materials of food, not to mention thousands of human lives." He derides this nineteenth century with its "Franklin-Benthamite religion," *i. e.* with rationalism for its profession of faith—"a vast prosaic Cockaigne of steam-mills for grinding sausages —for those who can get them. And all this in spite of all Manchester schools, and high and dry orthodox schools. Here were the strangest phantasms, new and old, sane and insane, starting up suddenly into live practical power, to give their *prosaic theories* the lie— Popish conversions, Mormonisms, Mesmerisms, Californias, Continental revolutions, Paris days of June. Ye hypocrites! ye can discern the face of the sky, and yet ye cannot discern the signs of the time!" When Lancelot, again, expresses his impotence of working for this end of social reconstruction under such unfavourable circumstances, his better genius, Barnakill, inspires him with confidence. "No," he says, "I dare not despair of you English, as long as I hear your priesthood forced by Providence, even in spite of themselves, thus to speak God's words about an age in which the

condition of the poor and the rights and duties of
man are becoming a rallying-point for all thought
and all organization." Further, when Lancelot, ready
to attempt the task, though with a sad heart, complains
that in the natural order of things he can hear nothing
but "the grinding of the iron wheels of mechanical
necessity," Barnakill replies, "Which is the will of
God. Henceforth you shall obey not Nature, but Him."

The heroes in both novels are idealists ; even Disraeli
can rise for a moment to the heights from whence he
can look down with noble disdain on party politics,
and spend some of his superb satire on partisan allegiance to a cause which only affects a fraction of the
nation, or humanity. "Come what may," cries Coningsby, "I will cling to the heroic principle. It can
alone save my soul." Both agree in this, that the
future of the nation rests with her young men under
twenty-five years of age, for both were the spokesmen
of two sections of young England at the time, and both
attribute an important share to feminine influence in
the work of social regeneration. "Women are the
Priestesses of Predestination," and this we presume on
the ground "that the surest means to elevate the
character of the people is to appeal to their affections,"
not to the material cravings of the Utilitarian School,
or the pure reason of the abstract political thinkers.
For, as the author of *Levana* says beautifully—"On the
blue hills of the obscure age of childhood, to which we
look back ever and anon, there stand out the figures of
our mothers, who thence pointed out the path of life

for us; and to forget that warmest of hearts is as
impossible as it is to forget the most blissful moments
of existence." This view of woman's place in the
social system and the work of social development and
amelioration is too little noticed by our modern writers.

But to sum up! Both in their divergences and agree-
ments the authors of *Yeast* and *Coningsby* point to one
great truth, which their novels abundantly illustrate
with all the wealth of a glowing imagination; in both
these novels we meet with given social evils which
demand specific remedies, and these are described
in almost identical terms, and traced to the same
causes. When two writers so vastly different in their
views come to conclusions so wonderfully alike, the
facts, at least, on which their reasoning is based must
be real, and to accuse one of these writers, as did the
chief organ of the Party of which Lord Beaconsfield was
the brilliant spokesman, of exaggeration and wilful
misrepresentation, was grossly unjust and unjustifiable.

But it is time now to turn to the actual proposals
of Charles Kingsley. At an early stage he proposed
emigration, land colonization, such as " General " Booth is
now carrying on in his " Home Colony," [1] and the like.
But, with the writers of the "Tracts by Christian
Socialists," he learned to regard them as mere palliatives
of the evils of competition. Reclaiming waste land was
another remedy which at one time had its attractions
for him; but in a letter on the subject written in 1858,

---

[1] See article on " General Booth's Farm Colony," in *Spectator*,
Sept. 12th, 1891.

and going into the matter in a very business-like manner, he points out the defect of this form of land redemption—

"It must be remembered," he says, "that if the land is waste, it is because it is poor, remote, or both, and therefore too expensive for profitable cultivation by the tenant farmers; and that therefore it will probably yield very ill, after a great outlay."

He suggests hereditary tenancies, for he had but little faith in spade husbandry—*la petite culture*—as generally understood, *i. e.* as identical with peasant proprietorship, for the want of capital in the latter case is a serious obstacle; he wants—an impossible ideal—to "restore the feudal system, the highest form of civilization—in ideal, not in practice—which Europe has seen yet." In the meantime, as we cannot take Time by the forelock and turn it backwards to "the good old times," he looks hopefully forward to the future, when "science should discover"—this was written in 1871—"some raw article of manufacture which can be grown freely on English soil, and which will require careful hand-labour—like the vine, mulberry, tea, coffee, cocoa, &c. Then, indeed, would the small farmer have a chance, *if he had saved money enough to start with in the meantime.*" Twenty years of further experience have not brought us much nearer to the discovery, and, unless we are mistaken, have not added considerably in swelling the working capital of the small farmer.

Here, then, and thus far, we have no proposals for heroic remedies. In the tract containing the substance of a lecture delivered in London, on the 18th May, 1857, shortly after his controversy in connection with *Yeast*, he sets forth at large his plans for the amelioration of the agricultural labourer.   The lecture was delivered on behalf of the Society for Promoting Working Men's Associations, and dealt with the "application of association principles and methods of agriculture."   A barrister who heard it, speaks of it in a letter to Mrs. Kingsley as "the manliest thing" he ever did hear, "and certainly never audience was kept for nearly two hours and a half so attentive, by the mere weight of the subject, and the force with which it was wielded." Here we must take Kingsley seriously; he deals with facts in a matter-of-fact way, and takes facts as they are.   The farm-labourers he has in view were not exceptional characters like Tregarva, nor the landlords models like Lord Minchampstead, but ordinary landed proprietors, with "no such stock of high farming maxims," with commonplace bucolics to work under them.   Taking them as he finds them, he reminds the former that all landed property is "held in fief of God," and that the Divine laws of conduct in the mutual exchanges of human service and commodities are superior to the laws of the market and commercial expediency, and that these "remnants of feudal and parochial socialism," by which he understands customary laws still acted upon now and then in country districts, "which some people are now so impatient to abolish, as interfering with the free battle between covetousness and the labouring man," are the very means of preventing the agricultural masses from sharing the fate of their houseless "white slaves" at "the mercy of Mammon" in the towns; that to destroy them is to open the field to cunning and cupidity, and a total disregard of justice in the contract entered upon between man and master. The Poor Law, from this point of view, is described "as an ingenious means of keeping the poor man a slave, without starving him into revolution." What he suggests as a remedy for the unsatisfactory relationship as at present subsisting between the employers of labour and their men, is association. He refers to Cromwell's method of draining, by means of associated labour, the fens of Cambridge-shire, which enabled him to found "the magnificent socialist organization, by which they have now become the fattest land in England." He gives a sketch, for which we have not room here, of the *modus operandi* in doing something of the kind now by large manufacturers; for example, establishing flax farms in a convenient spot, with a mill to work the flax when grown, "and round them locate, as thickly as possible, all mechanics and labourers employed," with a common kitchen and wash-houses for all, a common and well-organized system of sewage for sanitary purposes, and as a means of cheapening the cost of subsistence. Such an establishment he thinks might be made "chemically, as well as economically, self-supporting." It might be combined with the method of associating the labourers by means of profit-sharing. Thus you might create an industrial parish, with its library, club-house, co-opera-

tive store, and the rest, without interfering with individual rights, or breaking the laws of political
economy. This would come under the head of what
the French call *patronage*, in associated labour under a
head. But he has another plan, according to which ten
families of agricultural industrials might combine to
buy or rent land to be worked on the co-operative
principle. But, he concludes, nothing of this sort will
succeed without faith, and unless founded " on the rock
of everlasting justice"; and he adds, "I shall have more
hope in the long run, even of associate ignorance than
of competive wisdom, for justice without science is but
a poor blind child-angel, while science without justice
is a full-grown devil." Some may think that in all
this Charles Kingsley was too sanguine, and it has to
be acknowledged that attempts to carry out co-operative
farming thus far have not been crowned with signal
success, and in some cases have been attended by
lamentable failures. But the principles laid down in
this tract, and the motives furnished for their application in *Yeast*, have been more fully recognized every
year since they were published.

From the last report presented at the Co-operative
Congress at Lincoln in 1891, we learn that in 1890
there were 2022 acres of land in cultivation on co-
operative principles, with a working capital of £28,648,
and a rental of £2745. The profits amounted to £794,
the losses to £1155; but as to the latter, two societies, out
of twenty-two in England and Scotland, almost entirely
shared between them the losses; also it has to be noted,

that all societies holding less than ten acres are ex-
cluded from the list. The conclusion drawn from these
results is, that agricultural co-operation is on its trial;
that so far from dying out, eleven new associations were
created in the course of 1890. It is a proof of Charles
Kingsley's soundness of judgment to find, as the present
writer has discovered on making inquiries as to the
causes of the losses here indicated, that they were
mainly owing to the unwillingness of the societies to
pay for the best management; for, as his informant
puts it, "in order to get good results, they will have
to pay in a liberal spirit for the brains which were
supposed to manage it." This is the aristocracy of
talent to which Kingsley alludes in his tract above
referred to.

But apart from this, even within twelve years of the
publication of *Yeast*, in the preface to the fourth edition,
Kingsley could speak cheerfully of the progress made
in the improvement going on in agricultural districts.
There he speaks of the growth of self-help and independence among the labourers, of cottage sanitation
by landlords, and in general the country parson may
see "a rosier, fatter, bigger-boned race growing up"
around him than that ill-fed generation of 1815 to
1845. Kingsley also notices "the altered temper of
the young gentlemen," and an improvement in the
clergy in their mutual relations with the people, and
speaks of the social effects of the Anglican Movement
indirectly in developing not only a more stately and
reverent tone of mind in religious matters, but also

arousing the feelings of chivalry and Christian self-sacrifice; in short, a spirit "more genial and human than can be learned from that religion of the Stock Exchange which reigned triumphant—for a year and a day—in the popular pulpits." These roseate hues in the tincture of rural life and progress as here pictured are a little too highly coloured. Still, after making due allowance for the prepossessions and exaggerations of a mind, eager in its happy moods to see things in their brightest light, equally apt in its sadder moments to add shadows deeper than facts warranted, there can be no doubt that there has been some movement in advance in these directions.

Take, for example, the reforms recommended in the *Radical Programme* put forward under Mr. Chamberlain's patronage and approval a few years ago, or the proposals of one so well versed in agricultural subjects as the late Professor Thorold Rogers, in the short-lived periodical, *Subjects of the Day,* and making due allowance for the prepossessions and proclivities of the writers, we may be able to see how much remains to be done in the lines indicated in *Yeast.*

First and foremost among agrarian reforms is the desideratum mentioned by one and all of those who have given their attention to the subject—" *The object of all land reform must be the multiplication of landowners.*" And this, according to a writer in the *Radical Programme,* is to be effected in formally conferring on the State larger powers, such *e. g.* as the creation of small owners, a graduated probate duty levied on landed proprietors over a certain size.[1] Professor Thorold Rogers, in the article referred to, speaks of the settlement of agricultural labourers on such plots of land as the Act of Elizabeth prescribed, as "urgent," but he does not enter into details how it is to be brought about. "It is the landowners who made them social pariahs, and serfs without land;" therefore, says Mr. Rogers, quoting Cobden, "the English labourer has been divorced from the soil, and must be restored to it."

These are drastic measures to bring about the "golden age of agriculture," as Mr. H. George calls it, having his own well-known method of a single tax on land for effecting the same end, with which the author of *Yeast* could not have had much sympathy. But we are told in the last report of the Land Nationalization Society, there are signs of the spread of such and similar opinions both in Parliament and in the Press. In the religious world, too, we note a greater readiness to accept such theories. Papers like that read (and since published) by Mr. Albert Spicer at the Congregational Union of England and Wales, held at Hull in 1889, on "Christian Economics with reference to the Land Question," and the establishment of the "Land Restoration League" by a body of men representing the extreme wing of the High Church party in the Establishment, show a similar tendency in religious circles.

[1] "Occupying ownership and peasant proprietary established under certain conditions, by the aid of the State, acting through local authorities, seem to be the direction in which these objects can be attained."—*Radical Programme*, p. 127.

Next in order comes the subject of cottage accommodation, and that of improved dwellings for the operative classes in the country. These have received serious attention in the legislation of the last ten years, though strangely enough a writer on the subject in a recent article of the *Quarterly Review*—an unbiassed witness on such a subject—speaks of the condition of the labourers' dwellings generally as twice as bad as it was a century ago. The fact is, that owing to the obstructive tendencies of the local sanitary authorities, the Parliamentary Acts are rendered in many if not most cases inoperative. This, too, applies to the Allotment Acts, and the Allotment Amendment Act of 1890, which meet with the same obstruction even in the teeth of the scheme for carrying out "compulsory purchase at a fair market value," either for the purpose of cottage building or land used for allotments. The demand by the author of the *Remedies* nearly forty years ago, substantially repeated by the writer in the *Radical Programme* now, for at least half an acre of garden attached to each cottage, which, as the former pointed out at the time, would only require one acre out of seventy-two, or 270 out of an estate of 10,000 acres, to be divided for the purpose of supplying the labouring class with 760,000 in all, a modest demand enough, waits as yet realization, though noble-minded individuals have done as much and more without legislative direction or compulsion.

Thus, from a paper published by the Small Farm and Labourers' Holding Company, relating to Lord

Tollemache's cottagers, not many years ago, we learn
that in this case three acres of land are allotted to
each cottager, sufficient for the maintenance of a cow,
and it is "the cow," it is added, which "is the anchor
which fastens the labourer comfortably to his fair
haven." From Parliamentary returns it appears that
in 1886 the number of allotments detached from
cottages was 386,513, that attached to cottages 256,802,
i. e. a total of 643,315, for the estimated total of 800,000
agricultural labourers in England and Wales in 1881,
which is so far encouraging.[1]

From the Report of the Rural Labourers' League,
over which Mr. Jesse Collings presides, referring to the
Allotment Act of 1887, it would appear that in 1889
from some 8000 to 9000 men were assisted by its
means to obtain pieces of land, if not more, in one way
or another.[1] In the matter of small holdings the
Report of the Select Committee on this subject recom-
mends that five million pounds sterling should be
placed in the hands of the local authorities by way
of loan, to advance to intending purchasers three-fourths
or four-fifths of the purchase price, a certain portion to
be repaid, the rest to remain a perpetual charge on the
land, with a view to encourage the augmentation of
such holdings, as their diminution from natural causes
is matter of universal regret. A Bill introduced by
Mr. Jesse Collings to give effect to this passed the first
reading without a division.

[1] We quote from the *Times*, 27th July, 1887 ; see *Spectator*,
Oct. 12th, 1889.

All these are attempts, to use the words of Lord
Ripon on the occasion of founding the National Land
Company under the name of " The Small Farm and
Labourers' Holding Company," at an influential meeting
under the late Lord Carnarvon's presidency five years
ago, for " bringing the possession of land within reach of
the working-classes," as was also the suggestion made a
year or two ago, but not as yet acted upon as far as we
are aware, that the Church Commissioners should let a
portion of land under their control in small holdings,
with the same object in view.   It shows how much is
being done and considered within the limit of practi-
cability now, as the result of that awakening of the
public conscience following upon the appearance of
Yeast, though we are far from saying that the stirring
appeal made in it to landowners and the country
generally was the only or even the principal cause of
this awakening.

The publication of *Yeast* was one of the factors, and
a very powerful one at the time, though less so since,
in the general movement for the amelioration of the
working-man's lot in town and country, which the
circumstances and events as well as the passions of the
men, including the passion of philanthropy, set in motion
in 1848.   The author of *Yeast* shrank from suggesting
measures; he believed in the working of reformatory
tendencies in men, gradually bringing about practical
results in the work of the individual or the State.   In
this he was a true follower of Maurice.   But to give
direction to these vague tendencies and aims, it was

I

essential to state forcefully the data of the problem. In this he succeeded, and for this purpose the novel was an excellent and effective vehicle. Landlords, farmers, intelligent labourers, and not to omit the "intelligent public," all could here learn what was required to bring about a readjustment of mutual relations among the various subdivisions of the "landed interest" under its present altered conditions.

CHAPTER V.

ALTON LOCKE—THE SWEATING SYSTEM IN FICTION
AND FACT.

In *Alton Locke* Kingsley presents us with a picture
of the London artisan, and the hardships of workers in
cities, as in *Yeast* he sets himself to describe the trials
of the agricultural labourer. An enthusiastic friend
and former pupil speaks of *Alton Locke* as at once "his
greatest poem and his grandest sermon." Even so
calm and cautious a writer as Leslie Stephen says that
"*Alton Locke* may be fairly regarded as his best piece of
work." To these may be added the tribute paid to its
merits quite lately by a German critic, who, pronouncing judgment on the recently-published translation of
the work into German, remarks that, though written
forty years ago, it might almost be regarded as a
faithful picture of the labouring world now; and that,
moreover, as a realistic novel and in its power of social
vivisection, it contrasts favourably with more recent
works of fiction of the same description; that in the
faithful presentation of social distress and its power of
moving the heart to pity it even surpasses some of

these, such for example as Zola's *Germinal.* For here
the author in dissecting social maladies remains a cold
anatomist throughout, whereas in *Alton Locke* the warmth
of compassionate ardour is felt throughout. It is to
this predominating quality, no doubt, that the book owes
its popularity. Its vigorous and unflinching delineation
of suffering among the labouring poor, and its scathing
criticism of indifference and selfishness among the well-
to-do classes during that season of acute struggles, secured
for the book a place in the households of England. In
itself a book having for its chief contents the "self-
exenterations" of a tailor with a turn for poetry, using
what gifts he had for agitatorial purposes, was not
calculated to secure the favour of the reading world on
its own merits. But the fact that the dreams of the
tailor-poet, confused, inchoate, often wild in their weird
incoherence as here described, purported accurately to
represent the state of mind in the industrial world,
rendered the book attractive. Kingsley, with a remarkable amount of poetic insight, gave here an account
of the religious and social creed of a class whose inner
life was a *terra incognita* to the general public. He
wrote the book when still comparatively young, and
with a rare vividness of perception, seeing, as it were at
a glance, and interpreting with clearness and fidelity
for others what he had seen in the interior workings
of a working-man's brain. He succeeded in seizing the
chief characteristics of such a mind with the quick
intuition of genius. Here we have a description true
to nature of the intensity of hatred accumulated in the

heart of one thwarted in his endeavours to rise above
the dead level of his class under adverse conditions; of
his jealous querulousness at the artificial restraints and
restrictions of society; of the bitterness of spirit with
which such an one would regard the limitations of enjoyment in his own order compared with the liberation of
mind enjoyed by the privileged few.   Kingsley showed
how rancour and spite would supervene on finding how
under the most favourable circumstances and under distinguished patronage even the poor man of genius is
hampered, foiled, and frustrated in a world whose best
gifts are at the disposal of the wealthy classes; how
mental and moral superiority count as nothing when
pitted against the respectable mediocrity or even inferiority of those who are fortunate enough to be born the
children of parents in easy circumstances.   Kingsley
almost identifies himself with his hero in this.   The intensity of passion displayed in describing the struggles of
Alton Locke makes one feel that here we have a picture
of what Kingsley would have been and felt, had his lot
been to be born and bred under such conditions.   The rage
and iconoclastic fervour of the demagogue were there in
his own heart; though an aristocrat by birth and disposition, the opportunity was fortunately wanting to
bring it out.   This is the reason why he, in a totally
different plane of life, sees so clearly the attitude of mind
of one belonging to a lower social grade, and why he
describes so ably his inner experiences.   He himself
had lived them through in imagination.   He explains
himself in a letter to Thomas Cooper, a working-man

who had come under his influence, had joined the Christian Socialists, and was hated and misrepresented as a deserter by his former atheistic friends accordingly.

" The man who wrote *Alton Locke* must know a little of what a man like you could feel to a man like me, if the devil entered into him. And yet I tell you, Thomas Cooper, that there was a period in my life—and one not of months, but for years—in which I would have gladly exchanged your circumstantia, yea, yourself, as it is now for any circumstantia, and myself, as they were then. And yet I had the best of parents, and a home, if not luxurious, still as good as any man's need be. You are a far happier man now, I firmly believe, than I was for years of my life. The dark cloud has passed with me now. Be but brave and patient, and (I *will* swear now), by God, Sir ! it will pass with you."

The man who could in the overpowering sympathy of his impulsive nature write this in 1856, was the very man required six or seven years earlier to delineate with intelligent sympathy the feelings of the working-class in that important epoch in the history of English Industry. The book, like *Yeast*, was written under pressure in the busy winter of 1850. He rose every morning at five o'clock, writing until breakfast, so as not to let it interfere with his other occupations. It was the only book of which he made a fair copy, a proof in itself that it was not published in haste, though in after life he apologizes for its faults on the score of " my own youth, inexperience, *hastiness*, illusiveness." Parker refused to take it, as he feared the firm had suffered in reputation by the publication of *Yeast*.

Through Carlyle, Chapman undertook the publication. "And so," concludes the letter announcing the fact in Carlyle's most characteristic style, "right glad myself to hear of a new explosion, a salvo of red-hot shot against the devil's dung-heap from that particular battery." As Mr. Froude speaks in the second volume of the life in London of the depth of depression in Carlyle's mind at this time, it speaks volumes for the merit of the book he was thus favourably criticizing, that at such a time he could take pleasure in it at all. In after years Kingsley speaks of it as a venture which brought him in so much in hard cash. Comparing himself to others in the work of 1848, he writes to Thomas Hughes in his own head-a-go fun and frolic style—

"You fellows worked like bricks, spent money. . . . I risked no money; 'cause why, I had none; but made money out of the movement, and fame too . . . I made £150 by *Alton Locke*, and never lost a farthing."

But he proceeds, and we can believe him—

"And if I had had £100,000, I'd have, and should have, staked and lost it all in 1848-50. I should, Tom, for my heart was and is in it, and you'll see it will beat yet."

The fact is, like everybody else at this time, he strongly felt on the subject, and shared in the general consternation. "The truth is, I feel we are going on in the dark, towards something wonderful and awful, but whether to a precipice or a paradise, or neither, or both, I cannot tell. All my roots are tearing up one by one, and though I keep a gallant 'front' before the Charlotte Street people (*i. e.* the Council of Association), little

they know of the struggles within me, the laziness, the
terror. Pray for me; I could lie down and cry at
times." In this state of mind he wrote *Alton Locke*
and its little companion, the tract *Cheap Clothes and
Nasty*, which contains a still more fervent exposure of
the slop-selling system. The transparent sincerity of
both, coming as they did from his heart and going
direct to hearts capable of generous sympathy, soon
made them popular in the ranks of labour as well as
among the friends of the working-class. Rarely do the
labourers themselves, whether in town or country,
mistake the true ring of sympathy in one not of their
class speaking to or for them. The book, which was
written "for the sake of the rich who read, and the
poor who suffer," captivated both by its great earnestness and unmistakable enthusiasm. Kingsley speaks
of " abuse-puffs " in the press, and " dogs barking " in
the religious world, at the time of its appearance, but
in 1857 expresses wonder at the " steady-going, respectable people who approve more or less of *Alton Locke*,"
and the steady sale of his two socialistic novels. Fifteen
years later he received a letter from a " Chartist and a
cabman " from Brighton, thanking him for *Alton Locke*,
another from abroad who had read the book " in a time
of overwhelming misery," and found it the means of
saving him from ruin ; and yet again another letter
from a compositor in Leeds, who speaks of it as " the
means of preventing me from becoming perhaps one of
the dregs and scum of idle scoundrelism." Even from
Wesleyan missionaries in South Africa he received such

assurances of the spiritual benefit the book had proved to thousands in distant lands. The religious character of the book is unique as an attempt not only to show the connection between honest work and honest doubt, which has been repeated more than once since the publication of *Joshua Davison*, but as an attempt in fiction to show the reasonableness of Christianity as the working-man's creed. Kingsley makes it clear at the outset that he fully comprehends and appreciates the difficulties of belief in sincere sceptics of this class. " With the most of us, sedentary and monotonous occupations, as has long been known, create of themselves a morbidly-meditative and fantastic turn of mind," says Alton Locke somewhere, giving the natural history of unbelief in his own class. On the other hand, remarks the same person, " I cannot help fancying that our unnatural atmosphere of excitement, physical as well as moral, is to blame for very much of the working-man's restlessness and fierceness." And so it comes to pass that " they must either dream or agitate; perhaps they are now learning how to do both to some purpose." Yet at the same time, as Mackaye points out with his shrewd contempt of false pretensions, the very creed which has lost its power on the workman—" The moon of Calvinism, far gone in the fourth quarter when it's come to the like o' that," has left behind it the seclusive spirit it bred in the *élite* of the working-man, as their own organs in the press show abundantly. And for this reason he prefers to go back to Christianity pure and simple, as the true

religion of equality.   Kingsley is no believer in natural
equality, as he says in 1866, though he speaks of a time
when he held a different doctrine.   But if the period
of his life when *Alton Locke* was written is referred to,
it is hard to see how the writer of this book can be
said to be an advocate of the principles of 1789.   He
is here and throughout a believer in " the divine
equality of virtue and wisdom which is open to all
men in a free land," and therefore here more perhaps
than in any other of his works does he invite the
working-men to " try to take their place among ' the
aristocracy of God.' "

But we must go now to the novel to see this, and
it will not be out of place here to give an analytic view
of its drift and scope, with a few samples by way of
quotation from it which may throw light upon its general
teaching.   Alton Locke, a " sickly and decrepit Cockney,"
is the child of a broken-down small tradesman, who dies
early, and of a mother whose narrow creed warps her
mind and produces a stint of affection acutely felt by
the sensitive boy.   The religious atmosphere of home-
life is rendered stifling even to suffocation by the
frequent presence and sinister influence of one or two
of the least worthy representatives of the sectarian
ministry.   When he is old enough, his uncle, a prosperous man of business, puts him as an apprentice into
a West End tailor-shop.   Here the nauseous physical
surroundings, and the presence of elements threatening
moral infection, affect the delicate constitution of the
youth bodily and almost spiritually; but he is saved

from the worst by Crossthwaite, a hot-headed but true-hearted tailor journeyman and a Chartist.   He inspires Alton Locke with a thirst for knowledge, and in his pursuit of intellectual improvement the latter frequents a secondhand bookstall, where, with tears in his eyes, he is seen reading Bethune's life and sufferings.   The owner of the shop, Sandy Mackaye, by far the best-drawn character in the story, takes an interest in the lad, and becomes his guide in the study of books, and puts him through a course of Milton and Virgil by way of mental discipline.   As by degrees an intellectual revolution is effected by such readings, the ambition of Alton Locke is roused with a consciousness of power, encouraged by Crossthwaite's assurances that he is a born genius.   With it comes the dissatisfaction of struggling genius.

   " It came to me as a revelation, celestial-infernal, full of glorious hopes of the possible future in store for me through the perfect development of all my faculties ; and full, too, of fierce present rage, wounded vanity, bitter grudgings against those more favoured than myself, which grew in time almost to cursing against the God who had made me a poor untutored working man, and seemed to have given me genius only to keep me in a Tantalus' hell of un-satisfied thirst. . . .

   . . . Yes ; the Chartist poet is vain, conceited, ambitious, uneducated, shallow, inexperienced, envious, ferocious, scur-rilous, traitorous . . . . We have our time and you have yours ; ours may be the more gross and barbaric, but yours are none the less damnable ; perhaps all the more so, for being the sleek, subtle, respectable religious vices they are."

With the new ideas fermenting in his mind the last

vestiges of old beliefs, or fragments of faith, disappear,
concealment becomes impossible, and the declaration
of his sceptical creed to his mother leads to a final
separation, he is banished from his home, and finds a
refuge with Mackaye. Here he is visited by his uncle's
son, now an undergraduate at Cambridge, who takes
him to the Dulwich gallery of paintings. It is here
that he meets with his fate. It is the old story—"Who
is she?" A dean's daughter whom, with her cousin and
the stately Churchman, he encounters here as he stands
in raptures before a painting of St. Sebastian. The dean
takes notice of the artisan, whilst the latter has only
eyes for the young beauty, whose picture thenceforward
haunts his steps until nine years later by accident he
has another glimpse of her in Cambridge. In the
interval, like most young men in love, he writes verses
beginning with an impossible subject, is ridiculed by
Mackaye out of it, and is persuaded by the latter to
address himself to better things. He now, in company
with the Scotchman, hunts up the scenes where poverty
struggles with vice for a fit subject of a democratic
poet's muse. These scenes are described with all the
harrowing realism of which Kingsley's pen is capable.

"Those narrow, brawling torrents of filth, and poverty,
and sin—the houses with their teeming load of life, were piled
up into the dingy choking night. A ghastly, deafening,
sickly sight it was. . . . And stopping suddenly before the
entrance of a miserable alley—'Look,' says Sandy Mackaye with his Scotch grim humour, as Virgil might speak to
the author of the *Inferno*, 'Look! there is not a soul
down that yard but's either beggar, drunkard, thief, or

worse. Write anent that ! Say how ye saw the mouth o' hell, and the twa pillars thereof at the entry—the pawn-broker's shop o' one side and the gin-palace at the other— twa monstrous deevils, eating up men, and women, and bairns, body and soul. Look at the jaws o' the monsters, how they open and open, and swallow in anither victim and anither. Write anent that.'"

Equally powerful are the descriptions of the home of the seamstress, the "phalanstery of all the fiends." Personal observation, combined with a study of Carlyle and Tennyson, determines our young poet to apply himself assiduously to what he calls the democratic art of stating the people's case in measured rhyme, and this he does in close contact with the Chartist. The tailor-shop in which he works having been turned into a slop-shop, a strike is organized. It is in this way that Chartists are produced, we are informed. The men must call upon government to redeem their wrongs, and in order that this call may not be in vain, their voice must be heard in parliament. "If neither government nor members of parliament can help us, we must help ourselves. Help yourselves," says Crossthwaite, the organizer of the strike, "and Heaven will help you. Combination among ourselves is the only chance. One thing we can do—sit still. 'And starve !' said some one."

However, our hero discovers before long the weak points of Chartism. "Fool that I am ! It was from within rather than without that I needed reform. . . . For my part, I seem to have learnt that the only thing to regenerate the world is not more of any system, good or bad, but simply more of the Spirit of God." Mackaye advises the hero to proceed to Cambridge, and with his cousin's aid to work his way through the University. Here, as he arrives in the middle of a boat-race, he is made to meet the vision of his dream, Lillian, but also feels the distance which separates them, which leaves ample room for morbid reflections and resentful sentiment, which it must be confessed are a trifle unreasonable. However, literary hack-work is found for him, and with it an entrance, too, into the Dean's house, though a damper is put on the ardour of the young man when, listening with ecstasies as Lillian sings one of his own songs, the Churchman overhearing it says to his daughter—

" What's that about brotherhood and freedom, Lillian ? we don't want anything of that kind here."

Now the publication of his poems is thought of and effected with the help of the Dean, but not until, by the latter's advice, the more objectionable passages breathing Chartism and democratic sentiment are expunged. They secure a great success. Alton Locke now returns to Mackaye, who does not approve of this concession to aristocratic patronage. The hero's occupation now undergoes another change. He becomes a contributor to an inflammatory print, and writhes under the tyranny of the editor of the *Weekly Wharwhoop.*

" It was miserable work, there is no denying it—only not worse than tailoring." He breaks with O'Flynn, and this brings another humiliation on his head. The angry editor denounces him as a traitor to the people

in his paper, in thus mutilating his poems. To redeem
his character in the eyes of his workmen, Alton Locke
determines on a step which leads to his ruin. He
volunteers to go forth as a delegate into a disturbed
country district, which happens to be within easy
distance of the residence of his patron the Dean,
there "to preach Chartism to discontented mobs." He
attends the meeting convened for this purpose, listens
with suppressed rage to the wild harangues of some of
the speakers present, and, losing his self-possession when
his own more reasonable proposals meet with a surly
demand for bread, he exclaims, "between disappointment and the maddening desire of influence":

"Go and get bread! After all you have a right to it.
No man is bound to starve. There are rights above all
laws, and the right to live is one. Laws were made for
man, not man for laws. If you had made the laws yourselves, they may bind you even in this extremity; but they
were made in spite of you—against you. They rob you,
crush you; even now they deny you bread. God has made
the earth free to all, like the air and sunshine, and you are
shut out from off it. The earth is yours, for you till it.
Without you it would be a desert. . . Go and demand
your share of that corn, the fruit of your own industry:
what matter if your tyrants imprison, murder you?"

His speech in this tone of desperation produces a
result he scarcely dreamed of—a hideous riot ensues. In
vain he tries to stem it. A detachment of yeomanry
are sent for to quell it, and he as the supposed ringleader
is taken to prison. Then follows a vivid description of
the trial scene, and the horror and madness of the hero

condemned to three years' solitary confinement. From
the grated window of his cell he sees the new
church built for his cousin, who is at the bottom of
all this treachery which has led to his own downfall.
For it was he who informed the editor, and through
him his Chartist friends, of the facts in connection
with the volume of poems, and it is he who now, to
keep Alton away from Lillian, keeps the truth from
the Dean in connection with the hero's conduct on the
occasion of the riot, who would otherwise willingly
have effected Alton Locke's deliverance.   In the
bitterness of his heart, on leaving the prison he becomes
a confirmed conspirator.   At this very moment the
Chartist movement is reaching its climax, and Crossthwaite is in the thick of it.   Mackaye, who had discerned
its futility all along, dies on the memorable 10th of
August, when it came to a contemptible end.   His last
words are finely told in a scene full of tragic effect.
Eleanor, the cousin of Lillian, appears now in her true
character of a friend of the people's cause, though all
along Alton Locke had regarded her as an enemy.   From
her lips he hears what makes up the full measure of
his grief and shame, that Lillian is married to his
cousin.   Poetic justice is done by the latter's premature
death from fever, caught in the performance of his duty.
The hero, with the intention of committing suicide,
actually saves a wretch from it, Jemmy Downes, a
victim of the sweating system, now reduced by long
years of bad usage to the condition of the "gaunt,
ragged, sodden, blear-eyed, drivelling, worn-out gin-

drinker." Alton Locke accompanies him to his domicile, which is described with horrible reality, with the dead wife, whose unclosed eyes stare on the drunken husband reproachfully, and "on each side of her a little, shrivelled, impish child-corpse," with their arms round the mother's neck.

"Look!" cries the wretch, "I watched them dying! day after day I saw the devils come up through the cracks, like little maggots and beetles, and all manner of ugly things, creeping down their throats ; and I asked 'em, and they said they were the fever devils."

Shortly after this the speaker drowns himself in the poisoned sewer below. After the vials of wrath are thus poured out on our present social system in its foul effects on human bodies and souls, a rhapsody follows in the style of Lamennais' *Paroles d'un Croyant*. Eleanor once more appears on the scene, and directs attention to the Great Healer, who alone can renovate human society.

"She spoke of him as the great *reformer*, and yet as the true conservative ; the inspirer of all new truths, revealing in his Bible to every age abysses of new wisdom, as the times require ; and yet the indicator of all which is ancient and eternal—the justifier of his own dealings with man from the beginning. She spoke of him as the true *demagogue*—the *champion of the poor* ; and yet as the true king, above and below all earthly rank ; on whose will alone all real superiority of man to man, all time-justified and time-honoured usages of the family, the society, the nation, stand and shall stand for ever. . . .

" Look, too, at the great societies of our own days, which, however imperfectly, still lovingly and earnestly do their measure of God's work at home and abroad ; and say,

K

when was there ever real union, co-operation, philanthropy, equality, brotherhood among men, save in loyalty to Him— Jesus who died upon the cross ? . . .

"I see it—I see it all now. Oh, my God ! my God ! what infidels we have been ! "

So cries Crossthwaite, who has been listening all the while, and so the book ends with a confession of faith on the part of the Chartist, and unfeigned hope in the regenerating influences of Christianity as applied to society on the part of the reformer, and an appeal to the Christian priesthood as the chosen instruments for this purpose.

"If they would be truly priests of God, the priests of the Universal Church, they must be priests of the people, priests of the masses."

In short, "The people can never be themselves without co-operation with the priesthood ; and the priesthood can never be themselves without co-operation with the people."

The hero, by Mackaye's will, emigrates, and dies suddenly on his voyage to Texas just before the ship touches land, when the ink is as yet wet on the last page of the MS., which is supposed to contain the "*Autobiography of Alton Locke, Tailor and Poet,*" the book here under consideration. A strange end to a very improbable story, as stories go, no doubt, and this general air of unreality about it is its chief fault. This must be acknowledged unreservedly, that as a novel it is almost a failure, but not so as a propagandist work of fiction. In its presentation of fact it is a complete success. In the description of fetid and filthy workshops and fever dens of the sweaters, in its exposure of the causes which turned honest and peaceable workmen into conspirators, the author of *Alton Locke* did the work of half a dozen labour commissions, and did it much more effectually by appealing in fervid tones of passionate sympathy to the well-to-do people of his day, calling upon them to rescue their fellow-men from destruction of soul and body, and stimulating private and public philanthropy to set about and face the social problem with honesty of purpose. Complaints were made against " the bitter, indiscriminate, and unsparing indignation which is poured out upon the rich, the government, and the clergy " in its pages, though equally severe are the denunciations pronounced there against the irrationalities of Chartism. The tone of indignation is maintained throughout against the faults and shortcomings of all concerned. And in this tone of real and unfeigned righteous indignation, the strength of feeling displayed in the volume, lies its chief merit. A milder and more measured presentment of the case would scarcely have elicited such a response as that produced by it in the mind of the public. The world had been lulled to sleep by the drowsy commonplaces and " the discretion of dullness " in its trusted and authoritative teachers, and though at first it resented the " impatience of philanthropy " on the part of Kingsley in this book, it thanked him before long for waking it out of the torpor of self-indulgence and indifference to the welfare of the masses —" his influence was great in enthusiastic young minds in the fifties," says a correspondent who had felt its power, in a letter to the author written quite recently.

Kingsley himself, in a letter dated January 13th, 1851, to a clergyman in answer to criticisms on *Alton Locke*, shows what were his feelings and intentions at the time he wrote it.

"*First*. I do not think the cry ' get on ' to be anything but a devil's cry. The moral of my book is, that the working-man who tries to get on, to desert his class and rise above it, enters into a lie, and leaves God's path for his own—with consequences.

"*Second*. I believe that a man might be as a tailor or a costermonger, every inch of him a saint, a scholar, and a gentleman, &c.

"*Third*. The workmen are tired of idols, ready and yearning for the Church and the gospel, and such men as your friend may laugh at Julian Harvey, Feargus O'Connor, and the rest of that smoke of the pit. Only we live in a great crisis, and the Lord requires great things of us. The fields are white for the harvest.

"*Fourth*. By the neglect of the Church, by her dealing (like the Popish Church and all weak Churches) only with women, children, and beggars, the cream and pith of working intellect is almost exclusively self-educated, and therefore, alas! infidel.

"*Fifth*. We are teaching them to become Christians by teaching them gradually that true socialism, true liberty, brotherhood and true equality (not the carnal dead-level equality of the Communist, but the spiritual equality of the Church idea, which gives every man an equal chance of developing and using God's gifts, and rewards every man according to his work, without respect of person), is only to be found in loyalty and obedience to Christ."

And so forth. And the contents of a volume written on these lines was characterized by the *Times* of October 18th, 1850, as "wild and wanton teaching." Was the reviewer one of those "stupid, or careless, or ill-willed persons" referred to by Kingsley in the preface to another edition of *Alton Locke*, written in 1854, and addressed to the working-men of Great Britain, who in speaking of the thoughts and feelings of the hero "have represented these as my opinions, having as it seems to me turned the book upside down before they began to read it"?

The "more ponderous batteries" of the *Edinburgh Review*, as one of the writers in the *Christian Socialist* calls them, were directed mainly against the supposed economic fallacies contained in *Alton Locke*. Whilst acknowledging the importance of tackling with the social anomalies attempted here, it took exception to the heat of feeling and proportionate absence of scientific light in the arguments. Kingsley is described condescendingly as "a zealous and experienced parish-priest, a gentleman of great literary ability, of very impatient benevolence, and evidently of somewhat imperious and aggressive temper towards all who check his hasty conclusions;" whilst the work itself "abounds in passages of wild and unchastened eloquence; and amid much aimless declamation, and not a little language which Christian feeling and scholarly taste must alike condemn, it breathes through every page a profound and passionate sympathy with the sufferings of the poor." As to the matter, apart from the manner, it is pointed out fairly enough that the economic doctrine taught here is the importance of replacing competition and contention by co-operation and concert as the method of industry. But, said the reviewer, the principle of association as such is not a new discovery, nor in itself opposed to the teaching of political economy. At the same time, to hold it up as a social panacea could only end either in a chimæra or tyranny; "associations" (the spread of which the reviewer thinks would in itself be an excellent thing in raising materially, morally, and mentally the individual workman) "when they differ from practical partnerships must be either lost in the whirlpool of competition, or wrecked on the rock of monopoly." True, when society has been Christianized, association may succeed; but then, when this spiritual remodelling of man's nature is effected, it will not matter very much what industrial system is adopted; but until then, and so long as human beings remain practically what they are now, the multiplication of associations would imply a continuation of competition with its evils, whilst merging them all into one would imply the greater evil of monopoly. To this Mr. F. J. Furnivall replied in the *Christian Socialist*, showing that according to the rules laid down in their tracts, containing the rules and bye-laws of such associations, the price of articles sold by the different associations of the same trade and place shall be regulated by these associations, *subject to the control of the Central Board, in such a manner as to prevent either monopoly or unfair competition.*"

The Edinburgh reviewer had assured the Christian Socialists that they were only attacking the symptoms,

not the source of the social malady, and wrapping
round him the philosopher's cloak with imposing
dignity, he added—

"We cast in our lot with their more systematic fellow-
labourers who address themselves to the harder, rougher,
more unthankful task of attacking the source rather than
the symptoms—of eradicating social evils rather than
alleviating them."

To this Ludlow, under the signature of J. T. in the
Christian Socialist, replied thus—

"I believe the principle of socialism is one that commends
itself to the mind of every one who has first embraced it
with his heart, *precisely because it does* go to the root of
social misery, whilst the political economy of the day only
crops the weed at the surface; *because it does* deal with
causes, whilst that political economy only deals with certain
resulting formulas which it calls laws. . . . Socialism, by
taking account of those moral causes which the economists
neglect, by placing realities in the place of abstractions,
'labourers' and 'capitalists' in the place of 'labour' and
'capital,' shows how selfishness and dishonesty, or fair
dealing and public spirit, must ever vary that proportion."

And disclaiming altogether originality or novelty
in emphasizing the importance of industrial association,
he proceeds to say—

"We deny that we are introducing new elements or new
arrangements (except so far as it always is and always
shall be a new element, a new arrangement, a new commandment, to 'love one another'); we say that we are
developing the old and true elements, restoring the old
and true arrangements. As Madame de Stael said that
'freedom was ancient, and tyranny alone new-fangled;'

so we assert that brotherhood eternally precedes division, and love hatred; that brotherhood and love can alone remodel and renovate, division and hatred only deform and dissolve society."

It is not an easy task to defend *Alton Locke* on artistic grounds. The hero even compared with Stephen Morley in *Sybil* as a typical agitator is inferior in moral calibre, though Lord Beaconsfield found it expedient to spoil the character of the people's advocate for the purpose of establishing his theory, that the salvation of the working-classes must come from the aristocracy. Still less favourably does *Alton Locke* compare with *Felix Holt*, a more recent creation of the same type of aspiring artisan, who, in spite of his aims in leading the rabble, succumbs in the struggle, the force of circumstances being too much for him. George Eliot's radical is a more finely-wrought character, self-poised in a more eminent degree, less the creature of circumstances, resisting nobly, however ineffectually, the temptations of his trying position; as a son, for example, which "required the utmost exertion of patience, that required those little rill-like outflowings of goodness which in minds of great energy must be fed from deep sources of thought and passionate devotedness." There is a resemblance in the speech-making of the two heroes at excited meetings, with equally disastrous effects in both cases. But on comparing that of Felix Holt with that of Alton Locke, the moral tone of the former, it will be found, is the more elevated of the two. "I'll tell you what's the greatest power under heaven," said Felix,

" and that is public opinion—the ruling belief in society about what is right and what is wrong, what is honourable and what is shameful." So, again, in his divine discontent Felix Holt never reaches the bathos of irrational querulousness justly censured in Alton Locke, who, when he speaks of his aristocratic rivals able to gratify the wish denied him of looking on his lady-love adored from a distance, though he assumes " they could not adore, appreciate that beauty as he did," grows mad over the thought that the very garment he has been stitching might touch her dress, and *he* making coats for *them !* These are not Kingsley's sentiments, but what he supposed to be the feelings of the discontented artisans of his day. George Eliot cannot form such a conception of a working-man hero. " You are discontented with the world," says Felix Holt to Miss Lyon, " because you can't get just the small things that suit your pleasure, not because it's a world where myriads of men and women are ground by wrong and misery, and tainted with pollution." And yet George Eliot has much in common with the author of *Alton Locke.* She shares in full his contempt for " pushing middle-class gentility." But she is more tolerant to it and the weakness of the populace alike, raised above the arena of contending passions. Kingsley is in the middle of the fight, and almost enjoys it. Like his hero, he arrives after many and some futile struggles at the higher platform, where the lesson is learned that, in the words of Felix Holt, " the way to get rid of folly is to get rid of vain expectations, and of thoughts that don't agree with the nature of things." But here again it must be repeated that the intenseness and restless impetuosity of Kingsley, his "spasms of sympathy" with his own hero's position, and his identification with him, and the intellectual fermentation around him, became a force in the great struggle for the emancipation of labour at this time. There is confusion and excitement; Pegasus rides away at full speed with his rider; the author is overmastered by passion, and does not entirely master his art, it gets beyond his control. What is a fault in the writer of fiction is a virtue in the social reformer. This overmastering eagerness and earnestness tells on the sluggish public, captivated by one who takes the kingdom of heaven by force, and follows his lead for the time being at least. George Eliot's mental discipline and ascetic restraint in speculation does not permit her social sympathies full flow. She took an interest in the revolution of 1848, which was a social revolution in intention; but she speaks disparagingly in her journal of Louis Blanc, one of the principal actors in it, on meeting him in London society. We are told that she read industriously the writings of Robert Owen and Saint Simon, but they appear not to have made any profound impression on her severely analytical mind. The reverse of all this is true of Charles Kingsley. His mind is thrown into a paroxysm of excitement by the events of 1848-9, and in this state of mind he wrote *Alton Locke*. The time came when he cooled down, when in *Two Years Ago* he speaks contemptuously of

Fourier's *Casino-Paradise*. But this novel belongs to what has been called the reactionary period of his literary life.

A curious fact, proving how much the author in this book is merged in the social reformer, is the temporary absence of humour, for apart from the sardonic humour of Sandy Mackaye, there is an almost complete absence of this quality in *Alton Locke*. Kingsley was too much in earnest to give way to his natural tendencies, for no one can doubt that he possessed it in an eminent degree. But his humour forsakes him so that he cannot see the grotesque situations of his hero on more than one occasion. He himself was so sensitive to the sense of the ridiculous that on one occasion, at a meeting of the promoters, we are told, " he was quite upset and silenced by the appearance of a bearded member of council at an important deputation in a straw hat and blue plush gloves. He did not recover from the depression produced by those gloves for days." That one who attributed humour to the Deity, and who, in the *Saint's Tragedy*, belonging to the same period, serious as was its intention, introduces more than one humorous passage, failed to do so almost completely in *Alton Locke*, cannot be explained on any other theory except this, that he was too intense to note its absence. The creator of Dick Hammerhand in *Hereward the Wake*, and the writer of those humorous epistles to Thomas Hughes which are dispersed over the pages of his Life and Letters, was too shrewd not to see the absurd aspects of Alton Locke's character and sayings, but his complete absorption in the subject or moral of his tale was such as to deprive him, for the time being, of his critical acuteness and sense of humour.

We may ask now, How far did Kingsley succeed by reason of this very earnestness in advancing the cause he had taken in hand ? what progress has been made in the direction of putting down the sweating system ? what improvement in the conditions of that particular domain of labour which he attempted to reform ? and lastly, what advance in the adoption of co-operative principles in modern industry, in the direction of realizing the dream of " the organization of fraternity " ?

As to the first, we find from the report of the Chief Inspector of Factories and Workshops for the year ending 31st October, 1889, that in most of those " workshops wherein young persons are employed there is a manifest improvement in sanitation," and " that the employment of females has been for some time past more regular and fairly confined to legal limits " (p. 94). Still, it is admitted a few pages further on (p. 104), " we have thousands of domestic workshops, dark, dirty, over-crowded." Mr. C. Booth, in his cautious and elaborate method of induction, balancing the pros and cons of sanitary and material progress among the working-classes, tells us—" In bad sanitation, over-crowding, long and irregular hours, the life of the English home-worker too often presents the worst features of the ' sweating system.' " And again, " Good workshops are the exception ; many of them are in a very unhealthy condition, badly lighted, ventilated, and dirty." From statements such as these by competent and unprejudiced inquirers, it would appear that little progress has been made since Kingsley wrote *Alton Locke,* but it has to be remembered that our standard since then has been raised considerably, hence the disappointment is more poignant. Also we meet in the same volumes with other statements which show that there has been considerable mitigation of the worst horrors of this kind ; still, "allowing that many of the troubles attributed to sweating are not industrial, and admitting that those which were industrial are neither essentially connected with any system of employment nor to be attributed to inhumanity, still, the trades of East London undoubtedly present a serious case of economic disease, with painful and alarming symptoms." [1]

But it is encouraging to read in the same volumes, containing a mass of evidence on the existence of so many festering social evils in the very metropolis of European commerce and British enterprise—" I am inclined to think that if an inquiry such as the present had been made at any previous time in the history of London, it would have shown a greater proportion of depravity and misery than now exists, and a lower general standard of life." [2] And is it too much to say that this improvement is partly owing to the exertions of the Christian Socialists and the publication of *Alton*

[1] *Labour and Life of the People,* vol. i., East London ; edited by Charles Booth, p. 487 ; cf. pp. 214, 238, 487 ; vol. ii. pp. 313-14.
[2] Vol. i. pp. 593-4.

Locke? Kingsley himself in the preface to it, written
in 1854, speaks of the improved condition of things
even then; and in his preface addressed to the undergraduates of Cambridge, he congratulates them that
"for thirty years past, gentlemen and ladies of all
shades of opinion have been labouring for and among
the working-classes, as no aristocracy on earth ever
laboured before;" and he inquires, "Do you suppose
that all that labour has been in vain?" It was not in
vain. Probably the improvements had not been as
great as he supposed and wished to believe. Kingsley's
was a very sanguine disposition, and men of strong
sympathies are apt to become optimists in spite of
themselves.

In the introduction to *Two Years Ago*, Claude gives
expression to the most comforting sentiments of self-
congratulation on the great social improvement since
1846-8, the spirit of self-reform and self-education, with
the tone of morals raised considerably among all classes;
"as for the outward and material improvements—you
know as well as I, that since free trade and emigration
the labourers confess themselves better off than they
have been for fifty years." Charles Kingsley was not
one of those preachers of smooth things whom he
characterizes in *Alton Locke* as "daubing the rotten
walls of careless luxury and self-satisfied covetousness
with the untempered mortar of party statistics." When
in later life he could look back on his earlier struggles
with comparative self-satisfaction and composure, it is
only natural that he should give way to a pardonable

weakness in believing that the world around him was much more improved than was actually the case.

As to the progress of co-operation, he never was deceived on this point, in fact he never ceased to deplore its comparative failure. The application of the principles of association to commerce and industry must be a matter of time and slow development, and simply for this reason, that, as Kingsley and his friends constantly affirmed, that depends on the growth of the non-self-regarding principles in the human heart; that, in the language of *The Co-operative Manual*, "to harmonize the discords of conflicting impulses, and convert the scorching heat of competition into a life-giving, cheering warmth," reason, "the fosterer of invention and incentive to progress," is not sufficient, but "requires the assistance of some power capable of moving the will by the influence of emotion to chose to do what the reason points out as fitting to be done" (p. 18); that Christianity alone can inspire and maintain this sentiment and supply this emotional force. Even in that branch of co-operative industry, namely distribution, which has attained to a phenomenal success, this idea has been almost entirely lost sight of.

Kingsley in 1854 complains of this reluctance on the part of the workmen themselves to adopt the principle which alone can raise their class morally and materially. "How little have the working-men done," he says in the preface to *Alton Locke*, addressed to the working-men of Great Britain, "to carry out that idea of association in which, in 1848-9, they were all willing to confess their salvation lay." And, writing to John Bullar in 1857, he confesses with regret that " ' associations ' are a failure, because the working-men are not fit for them." But as for his and Maurice's schemes, a failure of a hundred of them does not alter his convictions.

" I shall die in hope, not having received the promises, but beholding them afar off, and confessing myself a stranger and a pilgrim in a world of *laissez-faire.* For this is my belief, that not self-interest, but self-sacrifice, is the only law upon which human society can be grounded with any hope of prosperity and permanence. That self-interest is a law of nature I know well. That it ought to be the root-law of human society I deny, unless society is to sink down into a Roman Empire, and a cage of wild beasts, as it very probably may—as it certainly will, if your theory is accepted, that God has meant one man to rule, and many to obey."

This is in complete correspondence with what is said proleptically by the would-be reformer's last words in *Alton Locke*—

" And I have succeeded, as others will succeed long after my name, my small endeavours are forgotten amid the great new world—new church I should have said—of enfranchised and fraternal labour."

We are very far from acknowledging failure in the attempts here referred to ; to establish a vital principle and firmly fix it on the public mind is a task which is not easily accomplished ; it wants time for maturing, and the progress of growth in ideas which run counter to human selfishness must be of necessity very slow : what appears to be failure is only like the slowness of movement which resembles immobility to a hasty onlooker.   The idea is gaining ground from day to day, that co-operation is destined to be the future mode of carrying on industry, that friendly association will take the place of militant industrialism, in a measure at least justifying the unfeigned faith of Charles Kingsley—

" Association will be the next form of industrial development, I doubt not, for production ; but it will require two generations of previous training, both in morality and in *drill*, to make the workman capable of it."

This was said in 1856 ; one generation has passed away, and the prospect of fulfilment is not as near by any means as the true friends of co-operation might wish—still there is no real reason to despair of ultimate success.

L

CHAPTER VI.

"PARSON LOT"—HIS FRIENDS AND HIS FOES.

AT one of the gatherings of the Christian Socialists in the house of Mr. Maurice during the years 1847-48, Kingsley, finding himself in a minority of one, said jokingly that he felt much as Lot must have felt in the cities of the plain, when he seemed as one that mocked to his sons-in-law. The name of Parson Lot was then and there suggested, and by him adopted as a *nom de plume*. Two years later, in one of the humorous epistles in verse addressed to his friend Thomas Hughes, and included, as is the above anecdote, in the Memoir prefixed to *Alton Locke*, Kingsley thus concludes with one of his most characteristic clinchers—"Says Parson Lot the socialist chief." It was in keeping with this mode of using expletives and using strong language vigorously, that at the Cranbourne Tavern, and in a mixed assembly, he threw back his head and folded his arms deliberately, exclaiming, "I am a Church of England clergyman—*and a Chartist!*" It was impossible for him to be cautious in speech. But when he added in "burning language" that for him the Charter did not go far enough, he proceeds to explain—

an explanation his opponents omitted to notice—"my only quarrel with the Charter is, that it does not go far enough in reform." By reform he meant *moral* reform from within, not the changes to be effected by any number of reform bills passed through Parliament. "I think you have fallen into just the same mistake as the rich of whom you complain—the very mistake which has been our curse and our nightmare. I mean the mistake of fancying that *legislative* reform is *social* reform, or that men's hearts can be changed by Act of Parliament. If any one will tell me of a country where a charter made the rogues honest, or the idle industrious, I will alter my opinion of the Charter, but not till then. It disappointed me bitterly when I read it. It seemed a harmless cry enough, but a poor, bald, constitution-mongering cry as ever I heard," &c. &c. "God will only reform society on the condition of our reforming every man his own self."

We have quoted this here in the forefront of a chapter which deals with Kingsley as a controversialist and a pamphleteer, or, as some would call him, a social agitator in the Press, for *Politics for the People*, and the *Christian Socialist*, in which some of these controversies were carried on, were organs of the Press for agitatorial purposes. In them Kingsley's name appears attached both to poetry and fiction. The story of the "Nun's Pool," which had some difficulty in being inserted in the *Christian Socialist*, after being actually refused admittance to *Politics for the People*, and such songs as *The Day of the Lord* and the *Eagle*, the latter written near the Rhine, and both suggested by the troubles of '48, but left uncorrected in subsequent editions of the *Poems*, belong to the poetry of passion. The tract on *Cheap Clothes and Nasty* cannot be called a model of reasoned eloquence, it is full of righteous indignation against the iniquities of the sweating system. Here Parson Lot, having his righteous soul vexed, forgets for the time being the advice of Ecclesiastes to young men, " to remove vexation from their hearts." He is eloquent, but his eloquence is unchastened; he gives the reins to his righteous anger. The effect it produced was instantaneous. Published in January 1850, it was followed by a practical application of its teaching in the following month, when the first Tailors' Association was opened in Castle Street, with Walter Cooper, the ex-Chartist, as manager. The opening sentence of the tract, now published with *Alton Locke,* so severely censured by Mr. Greg in the *Edinburgh Review* as a " Tract full of raving," gives the key-note.

" King Ryence, says the legend of Prince Arthur, wore a paletot trimmed with kings' beards. In the first French Revolution (so Carlyle assures us) there were at Meudon tanneries of human skins. Mammon, at once tyrant and revolutionary, follows both these noble examples—in a more respectable way, doubtless, for Mammon hates cruelty, bodily pain is his devil, the worst evil of which he, in his effeminacy, can conceive. So he shrinks benevolently when a drunken soldier is flogged ; but he trims his paletots and adorns his legs with the flesh of men and the skins of women, with degradation, pestilence, heathendom, and despair; and then chuckles self-complacently over the smallness of his tailor's bills. Hypocrite!—straining at a gnat and swallowing a camel! What is flogging or hanging, King Ryence's paletot, or the tanneries of Meudon, to the slavery, starvation, waste of life, yea, long imprisonment in dungeons narrower and fouler than those of the Inquisition, which goes on among thousands of free English clothes-makers of this day?"

Mr. Greg condescendingly extends his pardon to this and similar outbursts on the score of Kingsley's excited state of mind as it dwells on the wretched condition of the victims of the system he attacks so fiercely. But he is inexorable on the severe attack on competition.

"Sweet competition! Heavenly maid! Nowadays hymned alike by penny-a-liners and philosophers as the ground of all society—the only real preserver of all the earth! Why not of heaven too? Perhaps there is competition among the angels, and Gabriel and Raphael have won their rank by doing the maximum of worship on the minimum of grace. We shall know some day. In the meanwhile, 'these are Thy works, Thou parent of all good!' Man eating man, eaten by man, in every variety of degree and method! Why does not some enthusiastic political economist write an epic on "The Consecration of Cannibalism'?"

This was the unpardonable sin. A tract of this kind written in the present day by a man of equal calibre would be read with approval by thousands. In the form of a lecture at a popular meeting at St. James's Hall, it would be received with deafening plaudits by the benevolent, and probably form an avenue of success to an enterprising genius of modern philanthropy, since it has become one of the liberal professions, so great is the change in the public mind since then. The facts and figures placed side by side of these two very strong passages fully explain the tone of mind in which they were written; they also are an answer to Mr. Greg's insinuations that Kingsley had failed to make himself acquainted with the actual state of things before writing. The victims of the slop system are described from veritable accounts and personal observation; "like Ulysses' companions in the cave of Polyphemus, the only question among them is, to scramble so far back as to have *a chance of being eaten at last*. Before them is ever-nearing slavery, disease, and starvation. What can be done?" The respectable customers are warned not to enter "the temples of Moloch—their thresholds are rank with human blood. God's curse is on them, and on those who, by supporting them, are partakers of their sins."

His contributions to the *Christian Socialist* bear more the impress of cool collectedness than this tract, but in the very letter in which he suggests to Mr. Ludlow what subjects might be treated in it and how, he also gives reasons for only speaking his mind in this bold fashion.

"This is a puling, quill-driving, soft-handed age—among our own rank, I mean. Cowardice is called weakness; to temporize is to be charitable and reverent; to speak truth and shame the devil, is to offend weak brethren, who, somehow or other, never complain of their weak consciences till you hit them hard. And yet, my dear fellow, I still remain of my old mind—that it is better to say too much than too little, and more merciful to knock a man down with a pickaxe than to prick him to death with pins. The world says, No. It hates anything demonstrative or violent (except on its own side) or unrefined."

On this point Maurice and his disciple were quite agreed. Maurice had defended the flaming title of the tract, *Christian Socialist*, on the ground that in approaching the English public "we must not beat about the bush." He expresses his approval of the tract referred to above, and with all his caution on this subject recommended a bold plunge. Kingsley was not the kind of man to hesitate when thus bidden. With him it was not so much matter of principle as predisposition; he simply could not help himself; he was a born fighter, sometimes adopting the language of the camp for that of the forum, or that of still more sacred places, as when he says, "If you want to get mankind, if not to heaven, at least out of hell, kick them out." When he talked of the "Scribes and Pharisees in white cravats laying on men heavy burdens, and grievous to be borne, and then not touching them themselves with one of their fingers," he was apt to use forcible language which, though it might be necessary, was not welcome to those whom he struck hip and thigh. But then Kingsley in some occasional fits of self-humiliation would readily acknowledge his excesses, and calls himself, with a charming air of genuine self-conviction, a "foul-mouthed, hot-tempered man." But those whom his written words had wounded had no opportunity of knowing his penitential regrets, and no wonder some of the clerical organs were up in arms against him.

But the fair-minded critic may always find in the collocation of several passages in the same letter or paper, or whatever it is that Kingsley writes at the time being, a fair and balanced statement of the truth he desires to convey. Take, *e. g.*, Letter III. to the Chartists. He begins by saying that he and they are all longing for the same thing, namely, "*to see all humbug, idleness, injustice, swept out of England,*" and this is, as a matter of course, put into italics. Further down the page we read, "What are the things which you demand most earnestly? Is not one of them, that no man shall enjoy wages without doing work?

"The Bible says at once, that '*he that will not work, neither shall he eat,*' and as the Bible speaks to rich as well as poor, so is that speech meant for the idle rich as well as the idle poor."

He then, referring to the passage in the Psalms where we read, "He helpeth the poor out of misery," and concluding with the words, "The patient abiding of the meek shall endure for ever," exclaims, "Only, my friends, let it be '*the patient abiding of the meek,*' not the frantic boast of the bloodthirsty."

Throughout, an equal proportion of solemn warning is administered impartially to rich and poor.

In the pamphlet, *Who are the Friends of Order?* he complains, that for having adopted the mode of speaking their mind without fear or favour, he and his friends

were cursed by demagogues as aristocrats, and by Tories
as Democrats, when in reality they were neither. He
takes credit to himself and them as to the practical
good they have effected in showing how many in "the
upper classes of society" cared for the poor and the
working-classes.   "I cannot call it either a doubtful or
a contingent one (the practical good referred to), to
make ardent and discontented spirits among the working-classes more patient and contented, more respect-
ful to those institutions of which they have been taught
the value, and of which they have often, but too little,
experienced the benefit; to turn their minds from those
frantic and suicidal dreams of revolution which have
been the stock-in-trade of such men as Feargus
O'Connor, to deliberate and orderly self-improvement,
and the pursuit of honourable independence."

He showed how as Christian Socialists they were
"fighting for the very existence of that property and
that order which we are accused by some of en-
dangering."

We may now examine a few characteristic passages
in what we must call his controversial writings—we are
not touching here on theological controversy, and pass
over the most important of these between Kingsley
and Newman—to see how far the extremists on either
side were justified in some of their strictures.   We will
first take *Politics for the People*.   When he said here
(p. 58), "that the true reformer's guide, the true poor
man's book, the true 'God's Voice against tyrants,
idlers, and humbugs,' was the Bible," he certainly

laid himself open to the charge of using severe
language. But then St. James had done so before him.
If his opponents applied the description to themselves,
they must have had a poor idea of their own civic
virtues. None but tyrannical employers of labour, idle
good-for-nothings, or actual social humbugs need have
taken offence; surely not the respectable supporters of
the Quarterlies, and the two leading Church organs of
the day! But the rich are specially stigmatized, it
might be said, for the warning is addressed to them—
"The Bible . . . is the poor man's comfort and the rich
man's warning." Our Lord, if we are not mistaken,
utters similar warnings to the classes and comforting
assurances to the masses in the Roman province where
He preached His Gospel to the poor. But in the Third
Letter. of the series occur one or two passages which
might even set at rest rich fools, if any such there were
then. For there the idle rich and idle poor come in for
an equal share of condemnation, and the ranting humbugs under either description, as we have seen already.
Whether he chastises the "Mammonite" in *Cheap
Clothes and Nasty,* in a temporary state of unnatural
excitement produced by the revelations of the *Morning
Chronicle,* or whether he tells hard truths to his Chartist
friends, in either case it is done for the reason given
in one of his letters written about this time—

"A man cannot write in the fear of God without run-
ning against the devil in every step. He cannot sit down
to speak the truth without disturbing in his own soul a
hornet-swarm of lies. Your hack-writer of no creed, your

bigot Polyphemus, whose one eye just helps him to see to eat men, they do not understand this; their pens run on joyful and light of heart. But no more talk about myself."

Not unlike to one in many respects who occupied a similar standpoint in relation to the French, as did Charles Kingsley to the English public, Lacordaire, sharing with the latter the characteristics of tenderness, loftiness of character, and candour all combined with an intense manliness and studious love of solitude, he also shared the latter's fate of being distrusted and misjudged by his fellow-defenders of the Church among the clergy and clerically-minded laity. Kingsley differed from Lacordaire in this, that he had not the Frenchman's unbounded faith in democracy. His own standpoint was rather that of the noble Montalembert, the friend of Lacordaire, that of a cautious acceptance of democracy rather than a hailing of it as a God-sent boon.[1] He shrinks from making his children *banausoi*, insolent, scoffing radicals. "Ah," he writes to T. Dixon of Sunderland in 1866, "that more men in all ranks would chose the part which you and your lost friend have chosen! Then they could

---

[1] Père Lacordaire brought out a democratic Catholic organ, *L'Ere Nouvelle*, at the outbreak of the French Revolution, and when, on the 4th of May, the National Assembly appeared on the peristyle of the Palais Bourbon to proclaim the Republic, the tonsured monk who stood in the midst of them, conspicuous by his white cowl, was cheered enthusiastically as he descended the steps, and conducted by the populace in a sort of triumphal march to the gates of the *Corps Législatif*."—*Frederick Ozanam, His Life and Works*, by K. O'Meara, pp. 316-20.

look on the inequalities of position in this world as slight matters, while they toiled after the divine equality of virtue and wisdom, which is open to all men in a free land, and try to take their place among the aristocracy of God."

That Lacordaire and Kingsley should be suspected of ultra-democratic tendencies, shows the penetration of the religious mind on both sides of the British Channel; clerical obtuseness of this kind is not a thing of the past. Ozanam explains the reason in the case of his friend :Lacordaire. "Not a word was to be said against his orthodoxy, but the form and manner of its enunciation was *novel*, and novelty was next to heresy. Nothing was held in greater horror at archiepiscopal head-quarters than novelty." The same explanation may be applied to Kingsley's case. Moreover, in his case there was his "blessed habit of intensity," which bishops and archbishops and minor office-bearers of the English Church certainly do not affect, and cannot appreciate. When the Dons of Oxford grudged an honorary degree to Kingsley, they strongly anim-adverted on the tone of *Hypatia*. And of this work, which Kingsley said was written with his life-blood, he also writes to Mr. Maurice in 1850, "My idea in the romance is to set forth Christianity as the only really democratic creed, and philosophy, above all spiritualism, as the most exclusively aristocratic creed." The tone of *Hypatia* is much calmer in this respect than that of the earlier writings, when he was labouring under an exaggerated sense of the social danger in the

Chartist times, which both to him and Carlyle was
"our reign of terror," "a manifestation of the Supreme."
"The truth is," he writes from Eversley to his 'dearest
master,' "I feel we are going on in the dark, towards
something wonderful and awful; but whether to a
precipice or a paradise, or neither, or both, I cannot
tell. I could lie down and cry at times. A poor fool
of a fellow, and yet feeling thrust upon all sorts of great
and unspeakable paths, instead of being left in peace to
classify butterflies and catch trout. If it were not for
the Psalms, and Prophets, and the Gospels, I should
turn tail, and flee shamefully, giving up the whole
question, and all others, as *ægri somnia*." This is talking excitedly, but it was talking aloud his thoughts
without reserve. But reserve was then held to be the
greatest force of the English Church, the width and
height of the clerical neckties of that day symbolizing
that choking dignity of which the present Bishop of
Liverpool then complained the Church was dying. Let
us hear Kingsley giving his impressions of the Frimley
murder, which had a terrorizing effect on his own
neighbourhood. He writes in the *Christian Socialist*,
and under the pseudonym "Parson Lot," and shows the
connection between political economy and such excuses
arising from economic causes :—

"I believe political economy to be all but the highest
and most spiritual of sciences; the science of organizing
politics and of making men good citizens; of realizing out-
wardly the ideas of the Kingdom of God; but I will say
nothing about it now: I will simply ask, 'If you allow

us to use moral means to hop-pickers, why not to their masters ? If to the outward accidents and symptoms of the system, why not to the system itself ?

" If it be replied, you must not interfere between employer and employed,"

he says in return—

" These are not moral questions ; they are material facts, affecting material interests ; and a political economy which cannot alter these facts is not worthy the name of a science ; it does not even show us how to regulate those very material interests which it claims as its exclusive sphere . . . I believe that political economy can and will learn how to cure these evils, and that, in accordance with the formulæ inductively discovered by such men as Bentham, Ricardo, Mill, and Chalmers . . . . ' Nature is conquered in obeying her ' ought to be held as true in political economy as in chemistry ; and the man who tells us that we ought to investigate nature, simply to sit still patiently under her, and let her freeze, and ruin, and starve, and stink us to death, is a goose, whether he call himself a chemist or a political economist."

Professor Marshall or Professor Sidgwick could not object to this. They would use different phrases to convey their meaning. The " reigning school of political economy "—as it was then—Kingsley says further on—

" was furious with Mr. Mill and Miss Martineau for having, even in a single sentence, deserted the devil of competition for the angel of association."

The old system which simply made political economy a system of organized selfishness is falling to pieces, as Kingsley predicted, to him it was even then " *ready to vanish away.*" The fulfilment of prophecy has at all times been taken as a proof of the sacred mission of the prophet.

In the second volume of the *Christian Socialist*, in the story of the " Nun's Pool," Kingsley speaks rashly of the " wholesale robbery of the poor—a robbery the most shamelessly hypocritical, effected, not by the voice of the nation, but by a single despot, abhorrent alike to the laws of God and of human justice "—he refers to the alienation of the land from the people, and the secularization of Church property in the time of Henry VIII. In the first volume he had drawn a parallel between the Exodus of the children of Israel from Egyptian bondage, and the deliverance of the working-classes from their modern " tyrants." Here he is frequently using the expression, " aristocratic tyranny," and also some arguments more in the spirit of Cobbett than that of a man professedly "justifying God to the people " on Church of England lines. We do not attempt to justify these outbursts; the managers of the Christian Socialist organs evidently did not relish them. Kingsley is not quite himself here. At all events, he is not at his best; rather at his worst. There are papers on the " Long game " which display a fair knowledge of political economy fairly stated, and there are papers passing for " Bible Radicalism," which are neither a credit to his biblical scholarship nor his radical opinions. His reasoning is at low ebb here, though in the main his advice is good ; all he can counsel is for the workmen to associate.

That Kingsley's views and opinions, thus somewhat loosely stated, and evidently bearing the impress of over-hasty composition—the papers really were published in fragments, and the series which was left in some cases unfinished—were severely canvassed by his opponents, goes without saying. Nor did he lack vigorous defenders. The columns of the *Christian Socialist* were fairly opened to opponents, and one writing under the name of Tory Bill makes a vigorous attack on " Parson Lot and his principles," to which " Radical Tom " replies, but it is not necessary to repeat these sayings. Nor need we quote at length Kingsley's in this publication to defend the Christian Socialist movement against some attacks on it by the *Guardian*. " Why connect them (the Christian Socialists) with the suspicious word socialism ? " the *Guardian* had asked. " For this reason : because we do not regard men as so many weights, and an association as a mere aggregate of individuals ; because we consider that men are moral beings, and that earthly circumstances, work amongst others, are to supply a moral discipline ; because we believe that no endeavour really to raise their condition by connected efforts can be successful which does not proceed on the feeling of brotherhood, and demand the exercise of self-sacrifice ; that we learn, in the divinely-ordained religion of the family, a lesson which is to be carried out in the wider circles of human society ; because we are convinced that it is God's will that men should work together as well as pray together, for a common benefit and a common blessing."

And again, in a second letter on the same subject—
"There is now in England a mass, an ever-increasing
mass of unemployed labourers, supplying victims for
unprincipled and short-sighted capitalists, or filling our
gaols and workhouses ; try whether association will not
gradually assimilate this mass, and render it the strength
and not the poison, the blessing and not the curse of
our country." He shows how association—and this is
all he meant by socialism—is the fundamental principle
of any Church system. It is curious that the High
Church organ in close touch with the Oxford Movement had thus to be taught that the individualism run
riot in economics corresponds to the disintegration of
Church life, and the dissidency of dissent and in matters
ecclesiastical, that the tendency of Christian Socialism
is really a tendency in favour of organized life, and a
restitution of that corporate union which lies at the
foundation of any Church system. When, however,
the *Guardian* made a personal attack on Kingsley in
"a cruel article" on the republication of *Yeast*, and
accused him of teaching heresy in doctrine and morals,
Parson Lot fairly lost his temper, as Mr. Hughes tells
us, and answered, "as was answered to the Jesuits of
old—*mentiris impudentissime.*"

Kingsley was involved in another controversy somewhat later, which pained his sensitive nature a great deal
more. He had been asked to preach one of the series
of sermons arranged during the time of the first great
exhibition by the incumbent of St. John's Church,
Charlotte St., Fitzroy Square. Kingsley was unknown,

M

except by his writings, by Mr. Drew, who professed to have read them with great interest, and had begged him through Maurice to preach the sermon. He agreed, though at some inconvenience, and took for his subject The Message of the Church to the Labouring Man. It was suggested by Maurice, and met with the most cordial approval of the incumbent; no questions were asked and no guarantees given, and "Mr. Kingsley took precisely that view of the message of the Church to labouring men which every reader of his books would have expected him to take." His text was "The Spirit of the Lord is upon me, because He has anointed me to preach the gospel to the poor," &c. (Luke iv. 18—21); and in the course of his sermon he had said—

"I assert that the business for which God sends a Christian priest in a Christian nation is, to preach freedom, equality, and brotherhood in the fullest, deepest, widest meaning of these three great words; that in as far as he does, he is a true priest, doing his Lord's work with his Lord's blessing on him; that in as far as he does not he is no priest at all, but a traitor to God and men." And again—"I say that these words express the very pith and marrow of a priest's business; I say that they preach freedom, equality, and brotherhood, to rich and poor for ever and ever."

He pointed out the two kinds of liberty—the one to do as one pleases, which is false, the other to exercise moral freedom "to do what he ought," which is right; the two kinds of equality—"the false, which reduces all intellects and all characters to a dead level . . . . the true, wherein each man has equal power to educate and use whatever faculties or talents God has given him, be they less or more. This is the divine equality which the Church proclaims." Then he proceeded to distinguish between two brotherhoods—" the false, where man chooses who shall be his brothers and whom he will treat as such ; the true, in which a man believes that all are his brothers, not by the will of the flesh, or the will of man, but by the will of God, whose children they all are alike. The Church has these special possessions and treasures : the Bible, which proclaims man's freedom ; baptism, his equality ; the Lord's Supper, his brotherhood."

The sermon was listened to with profound attention by a large congregation, many of whom were working-men. At the close, just as Mr. Kingsley was about to give the blessing, the incumbent rose in the reading-desk and declared, " that while he agreed with much that had been said by the preacher, it was his painful duty to add that he believed much to be dangerous and much untrue." The excitement in the congregation was intense. The working-men could scarcely be kept quiet and prevented from hissing, and otherwise expressing disapproval ; the preacher bowed his head, descended the pulpit, solemnly and silently passed through the crowd, which thronged around him with outstretched hands and an eager " God bless you, sir." In the vestry friends met him to express sympathy, and by their special request the sermon was printed exactly as it was delivered. Kingsley returned much depressed to Eversley. Nor was this all. When a leading morning paper opened an attack on him as the "apostle of socialism," and this was followed up by a letter from the Bishop of London putting an interdict on his preaching in his Diocese in consequence of a report of the incident which had reached him, Kingsley replied respectfully, requesting suspension of judgment till he had read the printed sermon. Letters of sympathy came streaming in, but few from his brother clergy ; a meeting was held by working-men at Kennington Common to express their warm allegiance and sympathy. A proposal even was made before the Bishop's prohibition was withdrawn, to ask Mr. Kingsley to start a free church independent of episcopal rule, with a promise of a huge following. Of course it was not entertained. When the Bishop had read the sermon he withdrew in a gracious manner, in a personal interview with Kingsley, his prohibition, and a fortnight later the latter preached in his father's church in Chelsea. It may be as well to quote one or two more salient passages from this sermon to show why Mr. Drew got so unduly frightened of having conjured up spirits of revolt which in his panic he felt he must lay, though at the cost of courtesy and good faith.

"In Judæa," Kingsley had said among other things, " there could be no absolute or eternal alienation of the soil, but only, as Moses ordered, a lease of it according to its value, between the time of sale and the next year of jubilee. If I wanted one proof above all others of the inspired wisdom of Moses, I should chose this unparalleled contrivance for preventing the accumulation of large estates, and the reduction of the people into the state of serfs and day-labourers."

Again, in a similar spirit—

" All systems of society which favour the accumulation of capital in a few hands—which oust the masses from the soil which their forefathers possessed of old—which reduce them to the level of serfs and day-labourers, living on wages and on alms—which crush them down with debt, or in any wise degrade or enslave them, or deny them a permanent stake in the Commonwealth, are contrary to the Kingdom of God."

Again, connecting the symbolical act of the " mystical washing away of sin " in baptism with sanitary reform—

" How dare you, in the face of that baptismal sign of the sprinkled water, keep God's children exposed to filth, brutality, and temptation, which festers in your courts and alleys, making cleanliness impossible—drunkenness all but excusable—prostitution all but natural—self-respect and decency unknown ? . . . In that font is a witness for education and for sanitary reform, which will conquer with the might of an archangel, when every other argument has failed to prove that the masses are after all not mere machines and hands to be used up in the production of a wealth of which they never taste, when their numbers are, as far as possible, kept down by economical and prudent rulers to the market demand for members of Christ, children of God, and inheritors of the Kingdom of Heaven."

There may be a few clergymen still living—we think we have met them in the flesh, and it is a weariness to the flesh to meet them in what they are pleased to call argument—whom words like these spoken in *their* pulpits would frighten as much as they did poor Mr. Drew. But the less unintelligent among the main body of the clergy now would listen with composure if not with complete assent to such a discourse by such a man on such an occasion. Things have been said by speakers at Church congresses quite as strong, and have met with a favourable reception. Yet it must be acknowledged that there is something in the profound tone of a few of these passages of the sermon quoted above which go far to explain, if they do not excuse, the irrational fear inspired by them in the minds of slow and steady-going people in Kingsley's day. Yet he could be calm enough at times. When consulted, as he often was, by the council of promoters on questions which turned up from time to time, and in the settling of disputes, he was judicious to the last degree. Thus, *e. g.*, in the great lock-out of the iron-trade in January 1852, his opinion was asked on the subject. The promoters had been requested by the men on strike to help them in putting their case before the public. He counselled non-interference between the masters and the men.

" I think whatever battle is fought must be fought by the men themselves. The present dodge of the Manchester school is to cry out against us, as Greg did, ' These Christian Socialists are a set of mediæval parsons, who want to hinder the independence and self-help of the men, and bring them back to absolute feudal maxims ' ; and then, with the most absurd inconsistency, when we get up a co-operative workshop, to let the men work on the very independence and self-help of which they talk so fine, they turn round and raise just the opposite yell, and cry, ' The men can't be independent of capitalists ; these associations will fail *because* the men are helping themselves.' "

He insists though on the men combining or associating as the only power to raise themselves by, but "if they can't fight their own battles, no men in England can, and the people are not ripe for association, and we must hark back into the competitive rot-heap again." So, again, when he delivers himself on such a subject as intemperance, a subject on which so many are apt to show a considerable amount of insobriety in judgment and licence in expression, Kingsley's remarks are a pattern of judicial calm. Referring to a discussion of this topic in the columns of the *Christian Socialist*, he expresses regret at the amount of space allotted to the subject, and then goes on to say, "It seems to me, that if the teetotal party persevere in their new eleventh commandment, the thing can only issue, some fifty years hence, in a great social split between water-drinkers and beer-drinkers, each party despising and reviling the other. I regard this teetotal movement with extreme dread. I deeply sympathize with the horror of our English drunkenness that produced it. I honour every teetotaler, as I honour every man who proves by his actions that he possesses high principle, and manful self-restraint; . . . but I think temperance in beer, like temperance in clothes, is at once a more rational and a higher virtue either than sackcloth or water." Again, "I dread the spread of teetotalism — first, because it will beget that subtlest of sins, spiritual pride and Pharisaism. . . . Believe me, my teetotal friends, every gin-sot in London will help you at that work. The many always find comfort to their souls in the thought—' Well, at least, if we do not abstain, we know that abstinence is right, and we will prove it by compelling our teachers to abstain. So we go to balls and parties, but we won't let the parsons. We are married ourselves, but we are too pure to let the clergy be so. If we are sots, we will take very good care that only a teetotaler shall preach to us." The true remedies, he thinks, against drunkenness are two — sanitary reform, which by improving the atmosphere of the dwellings of the poor will take away the morbid craving for drink, and the establishment of "small associate home breweries," to escape the dangers of adulteration and public-house tyranny. The fanatics of teetotalism would not love "Parson Lot" the more for such prescriptions, nor for the warning with which he concludes, that those who try to prevent their adoption are "with whatsoever good intentions doing the devil's work."

Again, on a question as often approached with passion by both sides of the controversy, nothing can surpass the judicious tone in which he advises the advocates of woman's rights to act with tact and judgment. He writes from Chester in 1870 to Mrs. Peter Taylor, in reply to her letter respecting the "Women's Suffrage Question," and whilst expressing sympathy he adds,

" By pamphleteering we shall not win. Pamphlets now are too common. They melt on the debauched and distracted sensorium of the public like snow on water. *By quiet, modest, silent, private influence we shall win.*

' Neither strive, nor cry, nor let your voice be heard in the streets,' was good advice of old, and is still.   I have seen many a movement succeed by it.   I have seen many a movement tried by the other method, of striving and crying and making a noise in the street ; but 1 have never seen one succeed thereby, and never shall."

Hearing about this time that Charles Kingsley had withdrawn from the movement, John Stuart Mill wrote to him to ask the reason.   It was the mode of procedure of some of its advocates which had shocked him so that he refused to attend any more meetings, the only branch of the movement to which he continued to give his influence being that for the medical education of women, to which he had always attached the greatest importance.   In his reply he quotes Professor Huxley's words as expressing his own idea as applied to this subject—"'To reconstruct society according to science,' we must steer clear of the *hysteric element*," and he expresses his determination to set forth " in every book I write (as I have done in twenty-five years) woman as the teacher, the natural, and therefore divine, guide, purifier, inspirer of the man.   And so, perhaps, I may be as useful to the cause of chivalry, dear equally to you and me, as if I attended many meetings, and spoke, or caused to be spoken, many speeches."   This did not please the screamers for women's rights.

Probably in none of his utterances was he more self-restrained and cautious than in his addresses to women.   Was it from the very dread of excessive sympathy, conscious as he was, that with all his manliness he had more of the feminine element in his composition than was good for him, and that he had to guard against this weakness ? Take the following bit of calm and cautious advice in a lecture to ladies on ladies' work in a country parish, as a sample. Speaking of visits to cottagers, he tells them (advice not out of place in these days, when women are divided into "men's women" and "women's women")—

"*Let your visits be those of women to women.* Consider to whom you go—to poor souls whose life, compared with yours, is one long malaise of body and soul and spirit—and do as you would be done by ; instead of reproving and fault-finding, encourage. In God's name encourage. They scramble through life's rocks, bogs, and thorn-brakes clumsily enough, and have many a fall, poor things ! But why, in the name of a God of love and justice, is the lady rolling along the smooth turnpike road in her comfortable carriage, to be calling out all day long to the poor soul who drags on beside her, over hedge and ditch, moss and moor, bare-footed and weary-hearted, with half a dozen children at her back,—' You ought not to have fallen here ; and it was very cowardly to lie down there ; and it was your duty as a mother to have helped that child through the puddle ; while as for sleeping under that bush, it is most imprudent and inadmissible ?' Why not encourage her, praise her, cheer her on her weary way by loving words, and keep your reproofs for yourself ? Even your advice," &c., &c.

"Piety, earnestness, affectionateness, eloquence—all may be nullified and stultified by keeping a poor woman standing in her own cottage, while you sit, or entering her home, even at her own request, while she is at meals.

"Neither like the poor such unceremonious mercy, such

untender tenderness, benevolence at horse-play, mistaking
kicks for caresses.   They do not like it, they will not
respond to it, save in parishes which have been demoralized
by officious and indiscriminate benevolence, and where the
last remaining virtues of the poor, savage self-help and
independence, have been exchanged for organized begging
and hypocrisy."

No doubt as he grew older, like most of us, Kingsley
became, if not more reticent, at least more careful in the
choice of words and phrases.   His whole mind and soul
became more self-poised and quiet.   He had cooled
down, as it was but natural that he should do.   The
caloric temperament, like everything else in nature,
follows the law that dissipation of force which produces
heat is accompanied or followed by a cooling process.
Thus it was that he arrived at that stage when men are
apt to look back with some regret to earlier ebullitions
of feelings and methods peculiar to youth and early
manhood, but which the wisdom of old age has learned
to disapprove of.   And so he says in a letter to Ludlow,
referred to already, "For myself, on looking back I see
clearly, with shame and sorrow, that the obloquy which
I have brought often on myself and on the good cause,
has been almost all of it of my own fault;" and he goes
on to explain, "I mean the proud, self-willed, self-
conceited spirit which made no allowance for other
men's weakness or ignorance; nor, again, for their
superior experience and wisdom on points which I had
never considered—which took a pride in shocking and
startling, and defying, and hitting as hard as I could,
and fancied blasphemously, as I think, that the Word

of God had come to me only, and went out from me only."

The time came when Kingsley settled down, as he promised that he would when writing from the West Indies, "into the quietest old theologian, serving God, I hope, and doing nothing else, in humility and peace." But he really never became a reactionary in his old age, as young radicals are apt to do when they have become extinct volcanoes.

"To me, looking back at what he was when he wrote *Yeast* and *Alton Locke*," says one who knew him intimately, "the change seems rather the natural development of his mind and character under more or less altered circumstances, partly because he saw the world about him really improving, partly because by experience he found society and other existing institutions more full of healthy life, more available as instruments of good, more willing to be taught, than he formerly thought."

Some think that when he became a dignitary of the Church his expressions became more decorous, and his manner more acquiescent in the social facts which had assumed a less satisfactory aspect in his less prosperous days; that when his own struggles with fortune had been crowned with success he got tired of fighting the good cause for others. He himself is conscious of this, and thinks it incumbent upon him to explain it.

"If I have held back from the socialist movement, it has been because I have seen that the world was not going to be set right by any such rose-pink way, excellent as it is, and that there are heavy arrears of *destruction* to be made up before *construction* can even begin; and I wanted to see a little. At least I see that the old Phœnix must *burn*, before the new one can rise out of its ashes."

But this was written in 1855, that is long before his dignities had in the estimation of his detractors or critics spoiled him. Nor is this theory of theirs borne out by the calm tone of gentle regret and resignation breathing in his last contribution to the dying *Christian Socialist*—it had changed its name by this time into that of *Journal of Association*. There he bids farewell to militant Christian Socialism, not as a warrior laying aside his armour from lassitude and fatigue, or in the Achilles' mood of renouncing the scenes of conflict in which he delights no longer, but as a fighting man who thinks that for the present the season of combat is over, the battle must be suspended for a while, Fabian counsels must prevail.

" Let us say little and work the more, we shall be the more respected, and the more feared too, for it. People will begin to believe that we really know what we want, and really do intend to get it, and really believe in its righteousness. And the spectacle of silent working faith is one at once so rare and so noble that it tells more, even on opponents, than ten thousand platform pyrotechnics. In the meantime it will be no bad thing for us if we are beaten sometimes. Success at first is dangerous, and defeat an excellent medicine for testing people's honesty—for setting them earnestly to work, to see what they want, and what are the best methods of attaining it. Our sound thrashings as a nation in the first French war were the making of our armies ; and it is good for an idea, as well as for a man, to ' bear the yoke in his youth.' The return match will come off, and many who are now our foes will then be our friends ; and in the meantime—

"The proper impulse has been given,
    Wait a little longer."—*Parson Lot.*

This was his last signature under that name. He
wrote at the same time to the editor, "If you want an
Epicedium, I send one. It is written in a hurry, so if
you like, reject it; but I have tried to get the maximum
of terseness and melody."   As it marks the close of the
career of the *Christian Socialist,* so it may fitly be quoted
here, at the close of the chapter—

"So die, thou child of stormy dawn,
    Thou winter flower, forlorn of nurse ;
    Chilled early by the bigot's curse,
The pedant's frown, the worldling's yawn.

Fair death, to fall in teeming June,
    When every seed which drops to earth
    Takes root and wins a second birth
From streaming shower and gleaming moon.

Fall warm, fall fast, thou mellow rain ;
    Thou rain of God, make fat the land ;
    That roots, which parch in burning saul,
May bud to flower and fruit again ;

To grace, perchance, a fairer morn
    In mighty lands beyond the sea,
    While honour falls to such as we,
From hearts of heroes yet unborn,

Who in the light of fuller day,
    Of loving science, holier laws,
    Bless us, faint heralds of their cause,
Dim beacons of their glorious way.

Failure ?—while tide-floods rise and boil
    Round cape and isle, in port and cave
    Resistless, star-led from above ;
What though our tiny wave recoil ? "

                                         CHARLES KINGSLEY.
June 9, 1852.

CHAPTER VII.

KINGSLEY AND CARLYLE.

" I CANNOT say what I personally owe to that man's writings," says Charles Kingsley, in a letter addressed to Thomas Cooper, and dated Feb. 15th, 1850. It is not by any means the only passage in the *Letters and Memories* acknowledging this indebtedness to Carlyle. However, it is not so much our purpose to show how far this indebtedness extends as it is to indicate the joint labours of Carlyle and Kingsley in their work of social reform, mainly through literature, each working in his own sphere, though in a measure as master and disciple respectively. Carlyle was "full of thoughts on the great social question of the day," as far back as 1828,[1] that is when Kingsley was a boy nine years old. But the doctrines taught in *Chartism* on the condition-of-England question, published eleven years later, and devoured by the young Kingsley with all the ardour of early impressionableness, may be seen faithfully reflected in the pages of *Alton Locke*—" Carlyle is an old Hebrew prophet, who goes to prince and beggar, and says, ' If

[1] *Thomas Carlyle:* a history of the first forty years of his life, by J. A. Froude, vol. ii. p. 60.

you do this or that, you will go to hell—not the hell that the priests talk of, but a hell on this earth,'" said Kingsley to a Cambridge College friend. It was this touch of sympathy with Hebraistic intenseness which accounts for the kinship of the two souls, moving in worlds apart, and moulded by different influences from beginning to end. How well Kingsley understood the chief characteristics of Carlyle is evident from the life-drawing he gives of him in the person of Sandy Mackaye, though, strangely enough, Carlyle failed to recognize himself in this portrait.

The two men, in spite of disparity of age and up-bringing, had much in common, more at one, perhaps, in their hates—both satisfied Dr. Johnson's requirements of a good hater—than their loves, their dislikes than their likes. Both from their very soul loathed conventionality and cant, both were ardent in their attachment to truth and plain-speaking, and often overdid this. Both, though friends of the people, were the friends of order, but very far from joining the common cry about " order and progress." Both had a touch of Imperialism in their composition, and for this reason perhaps were a trifle too much frightened by " our French Revolution." Both abominated that real child of the Revolution, the doctrine of *laissez-faire*, and with it the egoistic mammonism it engendered; neither Carlyle nor Kingsley had any pity for the " plumpy, comfortable, pot-bellied reality of materialistic Manchester schools," and both appealed to the really spiritual side of human nature, and a higher altruistic ideal, and both waxed eloquent on the "Chivalry of Labour" that is to be, organized by the "captains of Industry." Both spoke of the supreme "sanctity of work" and the "holiness of suffering," and both were terribly in earnest in reminding their countrymen that there is a Providence presiding over the affairs of man, individually and in the aggregate. Neither believed in coercion to put down the "Chimera of Chartism," so long as "the living essence of Chartism has not been put down. Chartism means the bitter discontent grown fierce and mad, the wrong condition therefore, or the wrong disposition, of the working-classes of England . . . the essence continuing, new and ever new embodiments, chimeras madder or less mad, have to continue." Both addressed themselves to the task of speaking to and for "that great dumb toiling class which cannot speak." But neither was a believer in "Morrison's Pills" for curing social diseases; "for my part," Alton Locke says, "I seem to have learned that the only thing to regenerate the world is not more of any system, good or bad, but simply more of the Spirit of God." Inner reform is the thing required, not Reform Bills.

"The only progress to which Carlyle would allow the name was moral progress, the only prosperity the growth of better and nobler men and women; and as humanity could only expand into high dimensions in an organized Society, where the wise ruled and the ignorant obeyed, the progress which consisted in destroying authority and leaving every one to follow his own will and pleasure, was progress down to the devil and his angels." His only hope of avoiding the catastrophe was "a recovered sense of religion," [1] to teach the " sacred meaning of duty." For this reason even Carlyle acknowledges that "without a Church there can be little or no religion. The action of mind on mind is mystical, infinite; religion, worship can hardly (perhaps not at all) support itself without this aid." Of course it would be easy to point out divergencies and discrepancies and a difference of opinion in the numerous works of two writers, each possessed of a strongly-marked individuality, and each eminently original. But it is not our object in this place to point out the contrasts; let it suffice to note coincidences of thought and conjoint influences in their effect on the development of English thought and sentiment turned to social questions.

To enter a little more fully into each of the resemblances only hinted at above, we may now first dwell for a moment on the veracity of the two men, which constitutes their chief strength. " Veracity, true simplicity of heart," Carlyle says in *Past and Present*, " how valuable are these always! He that speaks what is really in him will find men to listen, though under never such impediments." And applying this to the subject in hand, he says in the essay on *Chartism*—" Infidelity to truth and fact and Nature's order being properly the one evil under the sun, and the feeling of injustice the one intolerable pain under the sun, our grand question

[1] *Thomas Carlyle:* London Life, ii. pp. 453-4; History of the first Forty Years, ii. p. 80.

as to the condition of these working-men would be : Is it just ? " Kingsley was a man of such transparent honesty, that Maurice on one occasion speaks contemptuously of any one who could even imagine his friend capable of innuendo—" the notion of accusing Kingsley of innuendo ! or of any language or acts but the most straightforward." This straightforward way of facing social problems in the Church and in the world, this honest effort of grappling with actualities and facing the supposed enemies of society with fairness of argument, is becoming nowadays more the rule than the exception, mainly through the surviving influence of these two writers, though the exceptions are still more numerous than we could wish them to be. There is still too much of that " pedantry and inane grey haze " in the inarticulate expressions, misty conceptions, and mystified utterances on the part even of the most outspoken friends of the people in their pronouncements on social questions, mainly because of the fear and dread of that intangible public opinion, which like a Damocles' sword seems ever hanging over their head.

Carlyle and Kingsley are lovers of order and harmonious organization, though both are not backward in sharply criticizing the "existing order," which they were apt to call disorder. Both agreed that a social order which was founded on a money contract and held together by selfish greed was no order at all, but anarchy, Mammon being the great Anarch; " that *laissez-faire*, 'supply and demand,' 'cash payment for the sole nexus,' and so forth, were not, are not, and will never be, a practicable law of union for a society of man."

They noted how the new industry by machinery which all the world worshipped was apt to turn men into "menials of the steam-engine," how multitudes of workmen, women and children, were sacrificed to this "huge demon of mechanism," that the poverty and misery of those thrown out of employment in any of the crises following upon reckless over-production were the real parents of "reckless unthrift, rebellion, rancour, indignation, against themselves and all men." What Kingsley had seen in Bristol riots, as a boy, Carlyle had noted in Glasgow, Birmingham, and even Paris and other places, as a youth, and in later manhood. They both could say, "we have seen and do testify," and they looked on with unprejudiced eyes. They clearly understood—the rest of the world with some few exceptions blinked the fact—that in the struggle for existence in what Carlyle called "this poor sordid era of ours," and Kingsley "this base generation," and the rest of the world "the age of progress," the weak must go against the wall, that freedom of contract becomes a hollow pretence where one of the contracting parties must work or starve, and his liberty consists in choosing between the two alternatives. They also saw nothing for it but some power to step in to protect the weaker party. Kingsley was less of a State-socialist than Carlyle. When, about the time of the Crimean War, the manager of one of the associations, at a council

meeting, asked Kingsley's opinion as to what should be
done in view of the impending bread-riots, and Kingsley
replied that one way was to let the merchants buy it
up and sell it six months hence, which answers best,
and the other was Joseph's plan, and when the manager
broke in, " Why didn't our Government step in then,
and buy largely, and store in public granaries ? "—
" Yes," said Kingsley, " and why ain't you and I flying
about with wings and dewdrops hanging to our tails ?
Joseph's plan won't do for us.   What minister could
we trust with money enough to buy corn for the
people, a power to buy where he chose ? "   And, we are
told by Mr. Hughes, " he went on to give his questioner
a lecture on political economy, which the most orthodox
opponent of the popular notions about socialism could
have applauded to the echo."

Carlyle, on the contrary, leans towards some form of
State socialism, though he is not very clear about it,
and his State socialism does not amount to much more
than a more real use and forceful application of the
existing powers and acknowledged principles of Government by way of State-aided education, emigration, and
the like.   What both aim at is what French and
Belgian writers understand by *patronage*, a return in
some form to a patriarchal relationship of master and
man, with the State *in loco parentis* where needed by
way of supplement, a real aristocracy of governors and
masters.

" We do say," remarks Carlyle in *Chartism*, and with
this Kingsley would be in full agreement, " that the old

aristocracy were the governors of the lower classes, the guides of the lower classes, and even at bottom that they existed as an aristocracy because they were found adequate for that. Not by charity balls and soup-kitchens, &c. ; in one word *cash payment* had not then grown to be the universal sole nexus of man to man ; it was something other than money that the high then expected from the low, and could not live without getting from the low. Not as buyer and seller alone, of land or what else it might be, but in many senses still as soldier and captain, as clansman and head, as loyal subject and guiding king, was the low related to the high. With the supreme triumph of Cash, a changed time has entered ; then must a changed aristocracy enter. We invite the British reader to meditate earnestly on these things."

He wants as does Kingsley more "Organization of labour." He sees the beginnings of a development of that new aristocracy he had demanded. He saw governments upset in France, and others raised in their place to do this very work of organizing "captainless" industry. But while he clamours for "Regiments of the new Era," and severely inveighs against "a blind loquacious pruriency of indiscriminate philanthropism," he after all calls for nothing else by way of Government interference than "a State grounding itself on veracities," not simply satisfied "with the most dexterous keeping of the peace," but establishing "*real* secretaryships" for "domestic peace and utility"—that is all. True, he says further on, "Suppose the State to have fairly started its *Industrial* regiments of the new Era," and got its "*men able to command* men" in ways of industrial and moral well-doing; "that the State would give its

very life for such men ; that such men *were* the State
. . . what a new dawn of everlasting day for all British
souls ! " But all this is *in posse*, and, if we are not
mistaken, is to be carried out in the works of national
workshops or model workshops by the State, for immediately afterwards we read, " Mill-operatives, all manner
of free operatives, as yet unregimented, nomadic under
private masters, they, seeing such examples and its
blessedness, will say : ' Masters, you must regiment us a
little, make our interests with you permanent a little
instead of temporary and nomadic ; we will enlist with
the State otherwise ! ' " What he really requires is a
mode of industry in which under the constitutional
government of the master or masters in the plan of
" constituted anarchy," the " poor blind methods,"
leaving everything to the free play of competition, are
to be abandoned, leading as they do to " Stygian
anarchy." Better too much government than none at
all ; the State must become " the keystone of a most
real organization of labour," for " it exists here to
render existence possible, existence desirable and noble
for the State's subjects." King Capital has proved
but a poor ruler. New kings and governors like
Cromwell and the great Frederick are wanted to rule
industry, a new order of nobles, " the captains of
industry," to support the throne. This in turn will
produce a new " chivalry of labour."

As to democracy, strange to say, Carlyle is much
more severe on its shortcomings than Kingsley, and it
is in the Latter-day pamphlets where he is most severe.

"Everywhere immeasurable democracy rose monstrous, loud, blatant, inarticulate as the voice of chaos." And what is this irresistible force, composed "of most inflammable, mutinous, chaotic elements"? What is this "huge inevitable product of the Destinies," this "big, black Democracy"? There lies the question for us. In trying to answer it, Carlyle speaks in what has been called the "Conservative Barricade style." Kingsley, with more moderation and tolerant breadth of thought, accepts democracy as a fact and a force, and sees the supreme need of Christianizing it. "The new element is democracy in Church and State. Waiving the question of its evil or its good, we cannot stop it. Let us Christianize it instead;" and he begs his correspondent to consider carefully whether "democracy . . . be not the pith and marrow of the New Testament."

In the extracts given by Mr. Froude from Carlyle's Journal (1830-2), it seems that at this time the rise of democracy was regarded with composure, if not with indifference, by him. "*La classe la plus pauvre* is evidently in the way of rising from its present deepest abasement. In time the world will be better divided, so that he that has the toil of ploughing will have the first cut at the reaping." Again, "Democracy gets along with accelerated pace—whither? . . I am purely an on-looker, in any other capacity there being *no need* of me." It is curious that twenty years later Carlyle should have assumed an attitude so much less in favour of the rise of democracy, except on the supposition that the revolutionary socialism of France and Chartism in England had disgusted him with democracy, which he thenceforward describes as a "self-cancelling business." Carlyle was a Girondist, and disliked revolutionary excesses. In his reminiscences of Lord Jeffrey this comes out still more clearly—

"Democracy, the gradual uprise and rule in all things of roaring, million-headed, unreflecting, doubly suffering, doubly sinning 'Demos,' come to call its old superiors to account at its maddest of tribunals; nothing in my time has so forwarded all this as Jeffrey and his once famous *Edinburgh Review.*"

Kingsley, innate aristocrat as he was, is not afraid of democracy. As late as 1872 he writes thus of himself to Thomas Cooper—"I can give no more solid proof that, while Radical cockneys howl at me as an aristocrat and a renegade, I am none; but a believer in the persons of my children, that 'a man's a man for a' that.'" True, unlike Carlyle, he never regarded Jesus Christ as "the greatest of all past and present *antigigmen;*" but he regarded Him as the great Regenerator of society.

"I have discovered also that the world is already regenerated by the Lord Jesus Christ, and that all efforts of our own to regenerate it are denials of Him and of the perfect regeneration which He accomplished when He sat down on the Right Hand of God, having all power given to Him in heaven and on earth, that He might rule the earth in righteousness for ever."

In this, however, Carlyle and Kingsley agreed, that is in looking forward to the creation of an "industrial aristocracy." "That," in Carlyle's words, referring apparently to Kingsley's expression, "a '*splendour of*

God,' in one form or another, will have to unfold itself
from the heart of these our Industrial ages too . . . an
actual new sovereignty, Industrial aristocracy." And
in order to this there must be higher ideals. On this,
too, both are agreed. The enemy of ideals at the
time was " Midas-eared " Mammonism, " pure egotism,"
with " try-to-get-on " for its shibboleth, and " devil-take-
the-hindmost " for its corollary, " the shabbiest gospel
that had been taught among men."

An able German writer, Dr. Gerhart von Schulze-
Gaevernitz, a friend and disciple of L. Brentano, in a
lately published work of considerable merit, on " the
social, political education of the English People in the
nineteenth century," gives a prominent place to Carlyle,
the " Isaiah of the nineteenth century," in counteracting
this tendency. He regards Carlyle as a spiritual force
to which more than to any other must be ascribed the
revulsion which has taken place in English thought
against exclusive individualism. Perhaps the author
rather over-estimates this influence of Carlyle's. For
the revulsion of feeling against the anti-social tendencies
of the past, and the profession rather than the practical
adoption of altruistic principles in the present day, are
the result of a general advance in European thought of
which both Carlyle's and Kingsley's writings were as
much consequence as cause.[1] Carlyle in the Reminis-

---

[1] See *Zum socialen Frieden. Eine Darstellung der socialpoliti-
schen Erziehung des englischen Volkes im neunzehnten Jahrhundert*,
von Dr. Gerhart von Schulze-Gaevernitz (1890), vol. i. 74-5 ; 87-9 ;
179 ; 235. The book is well worth studying.

cences mentions the year (1825) of his own Hegira
from the "soul-murdering mud-gods," when he attained
to spirit-emancipation from "Stygian quagmires."

"I have for the spiritual part ever since lived, looking
down upon the welterings of my poor fellow-creatures, in
such multitudes and millions still stuck in that fatal element, and have had no concern whatever with the Puseyisms, Ritualisms, metaphysical controversies and cobweb-
beries, and no feeling of my own except honest silent pity
for the serious and religious part of them, and occasional
indignation, for the poor world's sake, at the *frivolous,
secular, and impious part,* with their universal suffrages,
their nigger emancipation, sluggard and scoundrel protection societies, and '*unexampled* prosperities' for the time
being."

Henceforth he becomes the prophet fighting against
the infidelity to fact and unbelief in the Divine reality
behind the facts of the universe, against all unbelievers
in the Divine veracity, in their love for semblances and
"simulacra"; the "aim of the man of letters should be
to feel in himself, and reveal to others, the 'Divine idea
of the world'"; and so in a letter to his brother John in
1833 he says, "My mind would so fain deliver itself of
that 'Divine idea of the world.'" Starting from this
high conception of their mission and their message to
the times, both Carlyle and Kingsley cast to the winds
any considerations of private interest, determined once
and for all to "refuse to do the devil's work in this
which is God's earth, let the issue be simply what it
may. 'I must live, sir,' say many; to which I answer,
'No, sir, you need not live; if your body cannot be

kept together without selling your soul, then let the
body fall asunder, and the soul be unsold.'" Thus
Carlyle in 1837. Corresponding with this we read about
Kingsley, that when his friends urged him to withdraw
in 1848 from the sympathy with the people which was
likely to spoil his prospects in life, he writes to his wife—

"I will not be a liar. I will speak in season and out of
season. I will not shun to declare the whole counsel of
God. I will not take counsel with flesh and blood, and
flatter myself into the dream that while every man on
earth, from Maurice back to Abel, who ever tried to testify
against the world, has been laughed at, misunderstood,
slandered, and that, bitterest of all, by the very people he
loved best and understood best, I alone am to escape. My
faith is clear, and I will follow in it. He who died for
me, and who gave me you, shall I not trust Him through
whatsoever new strange paths He may lead me?"

For this reason both men, whose smaller failings and
human infirmities have afforded such an infinity of
comfort and consolation to the moral pigmies who are
ever ready to drag through the mud the great names of
men whose intellectual and moral grandeur they could
not measure, being the small-statured mortals that
they are, not only dwell emphatically on the sanctity
of labour—"He who has found his work," says both
Carlyle and Kingsley, "let him ask no other blessedness"—but they also emphasize the duty of self-sacrificing and self-denying activity. Society, from being an
agglomerate of self-seeking units chaotically thrown
together, must be restored to a belief in a Divine
Unity, and find here a Divine centre of Union. London

is to Carlyle a "huge aggregate of little systems, each of which is again a small anarchy, the members of which do not *work* together, but *scramble* against each other." . . . "Nevertheless, *God is in it.*" And so he emphasizes the fact in *Past and Present,* that the universe is not "a great unintelligible PERHAPS"; it is the same important truth on which Kingsley dwells in his novels, his lectures, his academical addresses. "In the heart of its tumultuous Appearances, Embroilments, and mad time-vortexes, is there not silent, Eternal, an All-just, an All-beautiful, sole Reality, and ultimate controlling Power of the whole?" Coming from Carlyle, such words produced a deeper effect than coming from a clergyman preaching on the text, "The Lord God omnipotent reigneth," for this is the idea which underlies all Kingsley's teaching, and on which he dwells most impressively, both in expatiating on the facts of natural history and the history of man. The fact is, these two men addressed in this respect two different constituencies on the same subject of supreme importance, each with its own prepossessions and convictions. Carlyle held up the belief in a Divine idea to the large body of men who had lost faith in the beliefs of their childhood, and were in search for a substitute. Kingsley addressed those who had their secret doubts, but were anxious to keep to the "old paths," or as near at least to the ancient landmarks as was compatible with truth. Both in their own way and in their own sphere did much towards restoring the faith in Providence, combined with a high sense of duty, and dis-

associated entirely from those emasculated makeshift
beliefs, which were virtually concealed unbeliefs, accepted
by men at the time.

Apart from the matter of their teaching, there was
much in their manner which was alike.   There are
fewer "splenetic sputterings" and "atrabilious utterances" in Kingsley than in Carlyle, but at times there
is the same impatient abruptness. He does not call
men contemptuously "Dead Sea apes," but he hits hard
at times, though with the velvet glove of gentlemanly
toleration.   But in both there is the same terrible
earnestness which Jeffrey used to complain of in his
kinsman contributor.   Both men had the faculty which
Carlyle ascribes to Shakespere, "that high *vates* talent
of interpreting confused human actualities," and both
use it for the purpose of drawing vivid pictures which
do not, indeed, unfold "what divine, melodious Ideals,
or Thoughts of the Supreme were embodied in them"—
for these were lost for awhile, they imagined—but
describe "the living chaos of ignorance and hunger,"
which was *the* actuality of the day.   Carlyle does so in
the sombre chiaroscuro of Rembrandt, Kingsley in the
rich colouring of Rubens.   Carlyle breaks out in a
"torrent of sulphurous denunciation," when he describes
the Past and Present Era of thirty years ago—"your
cotton-spinners and thrice-miraculous mechanism, what
is this too, by itself, but a larger kind of animalism?"
Nothing can be more severe than his strictures on the
"Pig Philosophy" of the age, nothing more solemn
than his warnings to turn away from such a degrading

materialism. Still, he is not quite hopeless. "Mechanism is not always to be our hard taskmaster, but one day to be our pliant, all-ministering servant"; "a new and brighter spiritual era is slowly evolving itself for all men." From the German, from Fichte in particular, he had learned to put his faith in idealism; and Christianity afforded him, as well as Fichte, the highest ideal for the individual and society. "Make an organ of *thyself*," says Carlyle, with the profound conviction that the higher development of the individual lies at the root of a higher social organization; and so he shows in *Characteristics*, which is "the most condensed example of Carlyle's peculiar teaching," that "society is the vital articulation of many individuals into a new collective individual," *i. e.* as we say nowadays, the individual is the cell of the social organism. Hence the importance, as Kingsley put it in his inaugural lecture on taking the Chair of History in Cambridge, "of the self-determining power of the individual" as a factor in the "orderly progress of humanity," denying the mechanical theory of an "inevitable sequence" in human affairs, which denies or ignores "the self-arbitrating power of man."

But *que faire?* What practical remedies are there to raise the individual and society, and for the present distress what ought to be done? They agree rather in what ought not to be done. Neither reactionary nor revolutionary measures will bring about a better state of things. Both dislike anything like an attempt to return to old and worn-out systems. Both

are bitter in their attacks on " Puseyisms " and
"Jesuitisms," the attempts in the Anglican and Roman
Churches to regain the people alienated from the faith
by attempts to improve their social condition à la
Cardinal Manning. In their strong prejudices they
were prevented from seeing any good in such sympathetic efforts, ready, as the Germans say, to throw out
the child with the bath-water.

On the other hand, Carlyle notes with his peculiar
sardonic humour the advances of " horny - handed
Radicalism." He notes with grim satisfaction its
earnestness. " Radical Murphy (at a meeting in the
City of London Tavern), with cylindrical high hat (like
a water-can), pot-belly, and voice like the great bell of
Moscow, All in Earnest." This was in 1834. A few
years before that Mr. Froude tells us he indulged himself in an " impatient Radicalism " of his own. But
when writing to Emerson he says—" Radicalism I feel
to be a wretched necessity, unfit for me ; Conservatism
being not unfit only, but false for me ; yet these two
are the grand categories under which all English
spiritual activity that so much as thinks remuneration
possible must range itself." Kingsley is much less
severe as a critic on Chartism, though his strictures
on its errors, as we have seen already, are pointed and
just. He, too, is equally averse to either reactionary
or revolutionary measures, and has as little faith as his
master Carlyle in mere accession of the masses to parliamentary influences and political power, or that the
possession of a twenty-thousandth part of a Talker

in our National Palaver will do "the people" much good. In fact, it is not political reform, but the inner reform of each man that is required in the opinion of both. To effect a happy union of society you must improve the social unit. It is a quite insoluble and impossible problem : *"Given a world of knaves, to produce an honesty from their united action;"* it is the moral not the political constitution that wants reforming; "it is not by mechanism but by religion, not by Self-interest but by Loyalty, that men are governed or governable." "Therefore," says Carlyle in his Journal, "'Society for the diffusion of common Honesty' were the usefullest of all societies could it take *effect.*" By honesty Carlyle meant a great deal more than keeping one's hands from picking and stealing ; he and Kingsley meant by this a more unconventional, more really outspoken honesty in speech and action, in religious profession, in moral practice. The current half-truths, morbid self-contemplation and weak self-pity, and utter inability to see straight and look facts courageously in the face, both men hated with a perfect hatred ; what they felt was needed were honesty of purpose and honest effort, eradicating the false, the feeble in thought and feeling. "The whole life of Society," complains Carlyle in the *Characteristics,* "must now be carried on by drugs; doctor after doctor appears with his nostrums, of Co-operative Societies, Universal Suffrage, Cottage-and-Cow Systems, Depression of Population, Vote by Ballot. To such height has the dyspepsia of society reached ; as indeed the constant, grinding internal pain, or from

o

time to time the spasmodic spasm throes, of all Society do otherwise too mournfully indicate." The myriads of mechanical inventions of a society, self-conscious of its sickly condition cannot save it, unless each member effects a personal cure in himself first. " To reform a world," says Carlyle in *Signs of the Times*, " to reform a nation, no wise man will undertake; and all but foolish men know, that the only solid, though a far slower reformation, is what each begins and perfects in *himself*."

But what are the prospects of this moral amelioration? On this point Carlyle and Kingsley differed. The former is inclined to Pessimism, though even in "chaotic London" he sees blissful symptoms here and there discernible of *palingenesia*. But at the very best he only clings to a desperate hope, for in his view the whole frame of society is rotten. Where the new is to come from when the old has vanished away he knows not, though out of all evil comes good, "this wonderous mankind is advancing somewhither," though " perfection of practice, like completeness of opinion, is always approaching, never arrived; truth, in the words of Schiller, *immer wird, nie ist;* never *is,* always *is a-being*." Allan Cunningham's " gingerbread Lubberland" is pleasant to him as "streams of ambrosial ditch-water;" yet says Kingsley, in justification of his own optimism, "All men worth anything, old men especially, have strong fits of optimism—even Carlyle has—because they can't help hoping, and sometimes feeling, that the world is going right, and will go right, not your way, or any way, but its own way.

Yes, we've all tried our Holloway's Pills, Tom, to cure all the ills of the world, and we've all found out, I hope, by this time, that the tough old world has more in its inside than any Holloway's Pills will clear out." He himself had learned to disbelieve in the efficacy of the specific, but had not lost his faith in the panacea for all human ills, the remedial power of Christianity, and the Church of England as an institution for the promotion of righteousness, individual and social. "Strange to say," he says in a letter to Captain Alston in 1862, "Thomas Carlyle now says that the Church of England is the most rational thing he sees now going, and that it is the duty of every wise man to support it to the uttermost." Perhaps Carlyle did not mean quite as much as is implied here. "That thing, the Church of England," as at one time he had spoken of it with supreme contempt, could scarcely have risen in his estimation to such an extent as to warrant this saying of Kingsley's. Towards the close of his life, we are told by Mr. Froude, Carlyle was taken by a friend to the Abbey to hear a great and popular preacher—was it Kingsley?—but before the service was over the friend began to regret his temerity in acting as bear-keeper to such a man in such a place. For every moment as the sermon went on its way, Carlyle's stick threatened to drop on the pavement to give expression to the holder's dissent and disapproval of it. Even the genial dean close by watched with some apprehension the movements of his friend, though happily the threatened signals of disagreement were not given, to the great relief of all concerned; but the story is characteristic of Carlyle. It does not, however, go far to prove the completeness of his conversion to good Churchmanship.

In the end Carlyle and Kingsley fought shy of each other, we are told by Mr. Garnett, and we can understand this easily enough. In his younger days Kingsley had looked up to Carlyle, not only as a prophet, but as *his* prophet; but as Kingsley grew older, Carlyle, like some others, probably thought that worldly success had taught him to prophesy smooth things. His later writings would seem, to Carlyle's eye, to be too optimistic, apologetic, and in the nature of compromising matters when antagonism and contention would be more in keeping with the demands of truth and justice. Probably the only Churchman with whom Carlyle entirely sympathized—Maurice even was never quite at ease with him—was John Sterling, but then John Sterling had separated from the Church, which he had entered without due consideration. Carlyle respected his conscientious scruples; he himself had refused for similar reasons to join the Scotch Kirk.

Now John Sterling and Charles Kingsley bore many resemblances. There was in both the same velocity of thought and intellectual impetuosity, the same headlong alacrity in arriving at resolves and conclusions, the same impatient rashness and self-conscious sensitiveness; both had been attracted for a time by what Carlyle calls "the transcendental moonshine of Coleridge's Christian philosophy." There was the same bright ingenuity which pleased Carlyle so much—both had the bent of the artist and some of the traits of the saintly character. But there was this fundamental difference. Kingsley was physically vigorous, though he wore himself out prematurely by the "very excess of life" which in John Sterling brought on disease and death. Hence the greater joyousness of existence in Kingsley, which reconciled him more easily to life's contradictions. Sterling's life was to Carlyle "a tragical history, as all histories are; yet a gallant, brave, and noble one, as not many are." Kingsley's could scarcely be called so. Sterling had given up his "democratic philosophies and mutinous radicalisms," as Carlyle himself, as Kingsley had done. But though to Sterling, as to Kingsley, religion *per se* was an indubitable fact—as, indeed, it was to Carlyle—yet "the Sun" of "English priesthood" rising over "vast ruins and extinct volcanoes of his dead radical world" was, in the case of John Sterling, to sink again. In the case of Kingsley nothing, we are told by a Cambridge acquaintance, who knew him as the Professor of History, was more patent than his desire to pass for an orthodox English priest. The fact is, Charles Kingsley, like De Maistre and Lamennais, both of whom were diligent students and admirers of Tertullian, had something of the African's fiery spirit, and not a little of the style and forcefulness of the Punic apologist in his composition. So far as he shared the fiery temper of Tertullian, he was a man after Carlyle's own heart. But by degrees Kingsley became more reconciled to

the existing order of things, and had learned to tolerate
the shortcomings of current thought, and in a measure
tried to justify the age he lived in; whilst Carlyle
remained in opposition to the end of his days.

Kingsley, who in his younger days had called Archbishop Whately, the apostle of tolerance and the
exponent of political economy as taught then, "the
greatest mind of the present day"; Kingsley, who had
never for a moment swerved from his allegiance to
the large-minded and large-hearted teaching of his
"master," F. D. Maurice, was a man too broad in his
sympathies, too wide in his catholicity and all-embracing
affectionateness, too joyous in his undying hopefulness,
to satisfy the severe and stern demands of the Philosopher of Chelsea, in whom the intellectual hardihood
as well as the hardness of the Covenanter had left their
indelible mark. Kingsley, like his Major Campbell,
was "a man very tender and pitiful to weak women
and children, but very terrible to full-grown knaves."
Carlyle shared with him the latter; less so, if at all,
the former qualities of mind and heart; he had not,
or at all events he had in much smaller degree, the
softer, gentle, pitiful forbearance with human foibles
and folly which his ci-devant disciple possessed in
an eminent degree. The peculiarities of character
come out most distinctly in the view the two men
take of *heroes*. To Carlyle the *sincere man* is the true,
"a veritable hero, if he prove a true man!" Kingsley
was attracted, as we see in his essay on Heroism,
"by the more tender and saintly ideal of heroism

which had sprung up during the earlier middle ages."
Stoicism, a self-poised self-concentration, is what Carlyle
admired most. "True heroism must involve self-
sacrifice," according to Kingsley. Therefore, however
unheroic the age may be, it is not necessary to be a
social Luther or a Knox thundering forth anathemas;
"any man or woman who *will*, in any age and under
any circumstances, *can* live the heroic life and exercise
heroic influences." Carlyle was attracted by the
stoicism of the English aristocracy. The reason is not
far to seek. Like the ancient, like some of our modern
stoics, he was himself an aristocrat morally and mentally
standing aloof from the common crowd. Kingsley, as
he showed in *Hypatia* and in the incomparable lectures
on " Neo-Platonism " delivered before a Scotch audience
—and Carlyle's cultured countrymen are apt to be
conscious of this moral and intellectual superiority
of the select few, an heirloom, perhaps, of the Calvinistic doctrine of election—is too deeply imbued with
the democratic creed of Christendom which permits
slaves and harlots to "gaze on the very deepest root-
ideas of their philosophy." " There was a truly practical
element here in Christian teaching; purely ethical and
metaphysical, and yet palpable to the simplest and
lowest, which gave to it a regenerating force which
the highest effort of Neo-Platonism could never attain."
Thus disparity of age, and growing diversity of views,
prevented that coalescence of opinion and harmonious
intercourse between these two noble-minded and faithful teachers of their day and generation, which would

enable a writer who admires both, each in his own way, to say of them, much as he should have wished to do so, that like Saul and Jonathan they "were lovely and pleasant in their lives, and in their deaths they were not divided."

CHAPTER VIII.

KINGSLEY AS SANITARY REFORMER AND PIONEER OF SOCIAL SCIENCE.

" I SEE one work to be done ere I die, in which (men are beginning to discover) Nature must be counteracted, lest she prove a curse and a destroyer, not a blessing and a mother; and that is, Sanitary Reform. Politics and political economy may go their way for me. If I can help to save the lives of a few thousand working-people and their children, I may earn the blessing of God." Thus writes Kingsley in a letter to J. Bullar, dated Nov. 26th, 1857. Of this work he never grew tired, and two years afterwards, when writing to Lady Harding, who had established a Convalescent Home for Children, shortly after the first meeting of the Ladies' Sanitary Association, of which from the first he was a warm friend and supporter, he says, " I am going to throw myself into this movement. I am tired of most things in the world. Of sanitary reform I shall never grow tired. . . . There can be no mistake about the saving of human lives, and the training up a healthy generation. God bless you and all good ladies who have discovered that human beings have bodies as well as souls, and that the state of the soul too often depends on that of the body." In his lecture on "Great Cities," delivered at Bristol, Oct. 5th, 1857, we note the transition state of his own mind from that of the social to the sanitary reformer, which also serves to illustrate the close connection between the two, for it was here in this very city, as we have already shown in a previous chapter, that he got his first lesson in social politics. The end of his social philosophy is a deep conviction that physics and ethics cannot be disassociated, that the tendency downwards in the moral grade and the social revolt in the working poor must in a great measure be attributed to material conditions. "They sink," he says in this lecture, "they must sink, into a life on a level with the sights, sounds, aye the very smells, which surround them." Even the craving for drink is owing mainly to the wretchedness of their domicile; "the main exciting cause of drunkenness is, I believe firmly, bad air and bad lodging." He dwells upon the importance of prophylactic measures to prevent the canker of social disease at the root; instead of finding wretched palliatives to remove the symptoms, he expresses his full conviction "that reformatories, ragged schools, even hospitals and asylums, treat only the symptoms, not the actual causes, of the disease; and that the causes are only to be touched by improving the simple physical conditions of this class; by abolishing foul air, foul water, foul lodging, overcrowded dwellings, in which morality is difficult and common decency impossible." This especially in view of the noble struggles under adverse circumstances of the poor themselves, "their stern, uncomplaining, valorous self-denial; and nothing more," he adds, "stirs my pity than to see them struggling to bring up a family in a moral and physical atmosphere where right education is impossible." He makes an earnest appeal to the philanthropic feelings of his audience, an appeal which, with others repeated under different circumstances and in different places, has borne some fruit in public measures and private beneficence. It amounts to this—"Let the man who would deserve well of his city, well of his country, set his heart and brain to the great purpose of giving the workmen dwellings fit for a virtuous and civilized being, and, like the priest of old, stand between the living and the dead, that the plague may be stayed."

A year later he writes again to John Bullar, expressing his determination thus :—

"I see more and more that we shall work no deliverance till we teach people a little more common physical knowledge, and I hail the Prince Consort's noble speech at Aberdeen as a sign that he sees his way clearly and deeply. I have refused this winter to lecture on anything but the laws of health ; and shall try henceforth to teach a sound theology through physics."

To Kingsley "a bit of sanitary reform-work is a sacred duty." Those who were pillars in the cause of sanitary reform then—Mr., afterwards Sir Edwin Chadwick, Sir John, then Mr. J., Simon, and "dear old Southwood

Smith"—were friends and correspondents. He did them good service in making the cause popular by his vigorous style of exposition and earnest exhortation, addressed crowds whom they could scarcely reach, still less persuade. Public opinion needed rousing on the subject, and public morality raising to a higher level. The pioneers of sanitary reform had to surmount numberless obstacles and at times virulent opposition to their efforts, for " the British nation," as Kingsley puts it, " reserves to itself, though it forbids to its armies, the right of putting to death unarmed and unoffending men, women, and children. . . . Public opinion has declared against the necessity of sanitary reform ; and is not public opinion known to be, in these last days, the Ithuriel's spear which is to unmask and destroy all the follies, superstitions, and cruelties of the universe ? " And again, " Sanitary reformers have turned again and again to her Majesty's Government. Alas for them ! The Government was ready and willing enough to help. The wicked world said, ' Of course ! It will create a new department. It will give them more places to bestow.' But the real reason of the willingness of the Government seems to be that those who compose it are thoroughly awake to the importance of the subject." Not so the mob of respectable people in town or country, the " comfortable classes," who are ever on the side of the great goddess, " Leave alone," and by whom the command, " Touch not the unclean thing," was most sacredly obeyed since it was the easiest thing to keep it. The time had not yet come for that identification of the causes of moral and physical evil which Mr. S. Laing, in his interesting work, *A Modern Zoroastrian*, tells us is the characteristic of the age we live in, and that "our most earnest philanthropists and zealous workers in the fields of sin and misery in crowded cities are coming, more and more every day, to the conviction that an improvement in the physical conditions of life is the first indispensable condition of moral and religious progress" (p. 224).

The visitation of the cholera was the most powerful ally since 1831 of the social reformers. But with its disappearance the fears it had provoked passed away from the public mind, and with them the anxiety to promote sanitation, though philanthropists, as Lord Shaftesbury's biographer tells us, "continued to preach the good doctrine that cleanliness is next to godliness," and conversely divines like Dr. Chalmers said "that the world is so constituted that if we were inwardly right we should be physically happy." Thus the Public Health Act was passed in 1848, by which a Central Board of Health was called into existence with Lord Ashley for its chairman, and Dr. Southwood Smith and Mr. Edwin Chadwick to support him—it was the latter who was the real *spiritus rector* of the Board. At first they were mainly engaged in taking measures to stay the invasion of the cholera and mitigate its horrors, especially in the following year. When appointed to this office, Lord Ashley writes in his diary, "It will involve trouble, anxiety, reproach, abuse, unpopularity.

I shall become a target for private assault and the public press; but how can I refuse?"

It was at this time that Kingsley preached the celebrated Cholera Sermons at Eversley, which were afterwards published, "peppered," as he says, "for London palates." In one of them, referring to the popular notion that the cholera was sent by God as a national punishment, for which the remedy suggested was the proclamation of a national fast and confession of national sins and repentance, he inquires—

"Did they repent of and confess the covetousness, the tyranny, the carelessness, which in most great towns, and in too many villages also, forces the poor to lodge in undrained, stifling hovels, unfit for hogs, amid vapours and smells which send forth on every breath the seeds of rickets and consumption, typhus and scarlet fever, and worst and last of all, the cholera? . . . To confess their sins in a general way cost them a few words; to confess and repent of the real particular sins in themselves was a very different matter; to amend them would have touched vested interests, would have cost money—the Englishman's god. It would have required self-sacrifice of pocket as well as of time. It would have required manful fighting against the prejudices, the ignorance, the self-conceit, the laziness, the covetousness of the wicked world. So they could not afford to repent of all *that*." And, therefore, "as soon as this panic of superstitious fear was past, carelessness and indolence returned."

He does not deny that the cholera is a Divine visitation, but he shows that it is a punishment for transgressing the laws of nature, the inevitable consequences of natural causes according to the irreversible decrees of the Author of our being.

"Yes, my friends, as surely and naturally as drunkenness punishes itself by a shaking hand and a bloated body, so does filth avenge itself by pestilence. Fever and cholera, as you would expect them to be, are the expression of God's judgment, God's opinion, God's handwriting on the wall against us for our sins of filth and laziness, foul air, foul food, foul drains, foul bedrooms. Where they are, there is cholera; where they are not, there is none, and will be none, because they who do not break God's laws, God's laws will not break them."

The Board, which had by its very efficiency incurred popular displeasure, that demanded the removal of Mr. Chadwick from his post, was reconstructed in 1858. After that its functions were divided between the Privy Council and the Home Office, with Sir John Simon for its medical officer.[1]

In 1866 another step in advance was made by the passing of a new Sanitary Act, which greatly strengthened the position of the central authority, but also provided for the supervision of all sanitary administration. Other Acts followed, all in aid of that "Sanitary Progress" which is so ably sketched in the article referred to in the note below, and more elaborately in Sir J. Simon's volume on *English Sanitary Institutions* (1890), on which it is based. For further particulars we must refer our readers to these publications, where, too, they will find statistics to show more completely

[1] See for more details an article on "Sanitary Progress" in the *Edinburgh Review* for January 1891.

the actual nature of the progress of sanitation made thus far.

Nor must it be forgotten that, politically speaking, sanitary progress is only "a single breaker in the general tide of reform," and has gone on *pari passu* with the progress of scientific discovery and its practical application. Of this close connection of science and the science of health Kingsley was throughout an eloquent exponent, as when in his essay, *The Air Mothers*, he incidentally dwells on the importance of teaching the rudiments of sanitation in public schools and colleges, as a branch of that social science with which the sons of the governing classes ought to be thoroughly or at least tolerably well acquainted. It is worth while mentioning here that Lord Shaftesbury, in his address as President of the Health Section at the Social Science Congress at Liverpool in 1858, stated that the preventible mortality of the country amounted to 90,000 annually, and it is gratifying to find the evangelical philanthropist uttering words which bear a remarkable resemblance to some sayings of Kingsley's on the same topic. " But when people say we should think more of the soul and less of the body, my answer is, that the same God who made the soul made the body also." In that very year Kingsley, in the essay which appeared in *Fraser*, appeals to all, in spite of " theological differences," to join in this " sacred crusade against dirt, degradation, disease, and death "; as, indeed, ten years before he had suggested that " sanitary league," of which Maurice, with his " dread of societies," did not approve, but one of which Kingsley's friend, Charles Mansfield, actually founded.   It is to these efforts of Kingsley's that Dean Stanley refers in the funeral sermon—

"Artisans and working-men of London," said the dean, "you know how he desired, with a passionate desire, that you should have pure air, habitable dwellings; that you should be able to show the courtesies, the refinements, the elevation of citizens, and of Englishmen."

And in this Kingsley's share—for there were not a few besides, like Sir Arthur Helps, who with pen and tongue helped on the work of sanitary reform—consisted as much in teaching others how to do it, as doing it himself.   This he did in his own vivacious and eager manner of embracing a cause, which helped in stimulating more sluggish natures, and producing a ferment of enthusiasm in quarters where such stimulants were required.   Thus in his speech on the " Massacre of the Innocents," at the first meeting in Willis's Rooms of the " Ladies' National Sanitary Association," he shows that the premature death of infants is not the " will of God," but " stupid neglect, stupid ignorance, or, what is just as bad, stupid indulgence " on the part of men and women, closing the speech in these forcible words addressed to mothers : " And will you remember that it is not the will of your Father that is in Heaven that one little one that plays in the kennel outside should perish, either in body or in soul ? "   At the Royal Institution, in a lecture showing the importance of applied science to the preserving of health, he shows

P

how if only parents would read and perpend such books as Andrew Combe's, and those of other writers on physical education, we should not then see the children, even of the rich, done to death piecemeal by improper food, improper clothes, neglect of ventilation, &c., &c. In his town sermons, such as the notable sermon preached in Liverpool on behalf of the Kirkdale Ragged School, he speaks of the "human soot" in a town where "capital is accumulated more rapidly by wasting a certain amount of human life, human health, human intellect, human morals, by producing or throwing away a regular percentage of human soot"; and warns his hearers, as he had done in his social novels, that as foul vapours destroy vegetation and injure health, "so does the Nemesis fall on man—so does that human soot, these human poison gases, infect the whole society which has allowed them to fester under its feet." At the same time he looks forward to a more scientific and more truly Christian era, when "our human refuse shall be utilized, like our material refuse, when man as man, even down to the weakest and most ignorant, shall be found to be (as he really is) so valuable that it will be worth while to preserve his health to the level of his capabilities, to *save him alive,* body, intellect, and character, at any cost; because men will see that a man is, after all, the most precious and useful thing in the earth, and that no cost spent on the development of human beings can possibly be thrown away." In the same tone he exhorts his hearers at the Chapel Royal, St. James's, in his sermon on loyalty, after referring to the fact that 200,000 persons had died of preventible fever since the Prince Consort's death a few years before ; and in allusion to the recent recovery of the Prince of Wales from an attack of the same disease, he exhorts his hearers to show their loyalty by attending to this duty of sanitary reform, which they owe to their sovereign, their country, and their God, until no fever alley or malarious ditch is left in any British city, so that through his exertions and theirs they " might deliver the poor from dirt, disease, and death."

Here Kingsley's scientific knowledge and habits acquired by scientific studies were of great advantage to him, and it will not be out of place to say a few words here on his scientific attainments, as a help to his sanitary efforts.

In all his lectures and addresses it was ever his aim to show not only this connection between science and sanitation, but also the intimate relation which existed between scientific studies and the practical conduct of life, between a knowledge of the physical and spiritual laws of human life. From a child he had a taste for natural studies, as his schoolfellow, Mr. Powles, mentions in his reminiscences incorporated in the first volume of the *Letters and Memories*, and this taste for science he retained to the end. Writing to Matthew Arnold in 1870, Kingsley says : " Ah, that I could see you and talk with you ! But here I am, trying to do my quiet work ; and given up now, utterly, to physical science— which is my business in the Hellenic direction." It is also worth mentioning here that these studies had a

sanitative effect on his own mind, keeping it from
falling into the snare of the fallacies of exaggeration
and exclusion towards which, by reason of his intensity
and emotional fervour, he was constantly gravitating.
Science taught him that reverence for fact which he
dwells upon constantly in his scientific lectures, and
also the importance of this inductive habit of mind.
And such were his powers of intense vision and
of dramatic representation in reproducing the vivid
impressions of facts on his own mind, that he could
state in a concrete and tangible form the most difficult
subjects of scientific import; therefore we venture to
express an opinion that Kingsley was really at his best
as a popular lecturer on scientific subjects.

One more trait in Kingsley's method of teaching
science has to be mentioned. He never dogmatizes; he
is suggestive, not doctrinal. "Find out for yourselves,"
he says to his hearers or readers. Thus in this very
lecture, after propounding several questions in natural
history which appear difficult to answer, he does not try
to theorize at all. "Who can answer these questions?
I answer—*Who but you*, or your pupils after you, if you
will but try." In the same way and before a more
critical audience, himself in the seat of authority, on
assuming the Cambridge Professorship, he says to the
crowd of listeners before him, "I am not hear to teach
you history. I am here to teach you how to teach
yourselves history." In this way he stimulates inquiry
and the spirit of adventure in quest of scientific
discoveries; and this, as he says in the lecture on

Thoughts in a Gravel-pit, "is the only way to get gold wisely, and spend it wisely"—*i. e.* by not being afraid of digging down deep for ourselves with open eyes for hidden secrets. "We will call our pit no more a gravel-pit, but a wisdom-pit, a mine of wisdom." His natural modesty, enhanced by scientific pursuits, comes out in a thousand ways; it was this which struck all that came across him, especially during his residence in Cambridge, sweet humility not being exactly one of the graces most cultivated by the average run of University tutors and professors.

And this modesty produces in him a reverence for scientific facts, which will in the end teach reverence for divine things, for nature reveals God. He attributes Carlyle's marvellous influence through his writings to the fact that they are "instinct with the very spirit of science," for in them he has taught men moral and intellectual courage to face facts boldly while they confess the divineness of facts; not to be afraid of nature, and not to worship nature; to believe that men can know truth; and that only in as far as they know truth can they live worthily on earth. Besides, there is nothing like a knowledge of unpleasant facts, for it leads to effort for the purpose of facing them manfully. If nature is the "spotted Panther," and many facts support this view, then, as panthers can be hunted down or tamed, so too nature can be brought into subjection by obedience to her laws. This has a sanitary bearing; physical evil can be prevented by a knowledge of therapeutic science, diseases can be cured,

and thus life saved.   For this reason he would establish
sanitary professorships in the Universities, and recom-
mends the study of natural sanitary science to boys in
the higher schools, and also a fund for the promotion
of " the teaching the teachers in common schools the
laws of health "; in this way, to quote the concluding
words of the ode composed on the installation of the
late Duke of Devonshire as Chancellor of the University
of Cambridge—

> " Spreading round the teeming earth,
> English science, manhood, worth."

Physical science, physical education, and their practical uses is his constant theme.   In a lecture to the
officers of the Royal Artillery (1872) on the study of
nature, he points out its important bearing on the
health of the soldiers committed to their care, and
shows how the men of science, though they do not wear
Queen's uniform, are fighting with the army though
against different enemies, against ignorance of the laws
of health, which causes death and disease.   He hints that
every officer in the army is really, or ought to be, a
health officer.   " The wise and humane officer, when once
his eyes are opened to the practical value of physical
science, will surely try to acquaint himself somewhat
with those laws of drainage and of climate—geological,
meteorological, chemical—which influence, often with
terrible suddenness and fury, the health of whole armies."

How far did Kingsley succeed in all these varied
efforts to promote the study of sanitary science ?   In
his beautiful essay on the *Air Mothers*, he himself

seems to anticipate slow progress in this direction, though it was written three years after the important Health Act of 1866, when, as Sir John Simon puts it, for the first time "the grammar of common sanitary legislation acquired the novel virtue of the imperative mood," and at a "moment of popular piety towards the cause of sanitary reforms." This, like all pious emotions in the individual and the community, is given to spasmodic efforts succeeded by relapses, and has to be stimulated into life again by appeals to the law if men will not obey the gospel. "We shall be," says Kingsley in this essay, "like the tortoise in the fable, and not the hare ; and by moving slowly, but surely, win the race at last." He was not very far wrong in his prognostic. But in the very year of his death was passed the Health Act, which had for its object "the consolidation of central functions," which enables the Government to watch over, assist, revise the action of local sanitary authorities, which promises fairly for the future progress of sanitary reform, and which made Lord Shaftesbury say with a sense of relief, Jan. 11th, 1875—

"Sanitary questions, of which I saw the dawn, and had also the early labours, are passed into 'Imperial' subjects. Boards are everywhere, laws have been enacted, public attention roused, and Ministers have declared themselves willing to bring to bear on them the whole force of Government. Not only am I not wanted, but my interference would be superfluous and an incumbrance."

We will not say that the voice of Kingsley was no

longer wanted after this public acknowledgment of the duty of the preservation of life on the part of the country and its Government. But it may be affirmed that the work of pioneering, in which he was principally engaged, had well-nigh come to an end. It is gratifying to read, in the article of the *Edinburgh Review* on sanitary progress, already referred to, the following sentence in allusion to statistics of sanitary results previously quoted—"These figures alone are an eloquent defence of the sanitary work which has been going on, for nowhere is sanitary progress so clearly seen as in a lowered death-rate for children of tender years." But, we are told, "the conclusion is irresistible that the sanitary progress of this country is sure, if somewhat slow." This is fully borne out by Sir John Simon's work on *English Sanitary Institutions*, and the two volumes of *Public Health Reports* by the same writer, re-published by the Sanitary Institute. When writing to this veteran of sanitary reform in 1854, Kingsley, complimenting him on his City Cholera Report, its cautious modesty, eloquence, and completeness, says, "I only wish that I may have half as fair an account of *solid work* done to render at the last account, as that report contains," and closes the letter thus: "Unless the physical deterioration of the lower classes is stopped by bold sanitary reforms, such as you have been working out, we shall soon have rifles but no men to shoulder them, at least to use the butts of them when required."

No one will agree with Kingsley in this modest

estimate of his own work in sanitary reform, and all will be glad to note the success which has crowned his labours.   There are those who have complained that Kingsley, in his excessive zeal for health of the body, approaches at times the border-line which divides the spiritual and fleshly schools of thought. But this is in complete forgetfulness that he always bears in mind the close connection between a healthy body and a healthy soul; as when he shows in the lecture on the "Science of Health," "that wherever we find a population generally weakly, stunted, scrofulous, we find in them a corresponding type of brain which cannot be trusted to do good."   So, too, in the lecture on the " Two Breaths," he points out the close connection between physical conditions and morality, how from ill-lungs we get not only bodily disease, but " folly, temper, laziness, intemperance, madness, and let me tell you fairly, crime."   For this reason he quarrels with the hermits, whose good qualities he knows how to value in a separate volume, but whom he dislikes because they looked upon " dirt as a sign of sanctity."

In 1857 he gives a sketch of possible sanitary improvements, which has since been filled up in Dr. Richardson's Presidential Address in the Health Department of the Social Science Association at the Brighton meeting in 1875, entitled in its printed form, " Hygeia, a City of Health."   Many of the things adumbrated by Kingsley at that remote date have actually come into existence, as the result of private or associated philanthropy or legislative measures, such as extended factory and work-

shop legislation, the establishment of public lavatories,
drinking fountains, public baths, gymnasiums, and pro-
visions made by urban authority so as to procure for the
masses pure air, pure sunlight, pure water, pure dwell-
ing-houses, pure food. Any one reading the two volumes
of Sir John Simon's reports during the course of his
official life, with the history of sanitary institutions,
showing what has been accomplished thus far in carrying
out the recommendations contained in those reports, or
watching recent efforts more fully to carry out the
spirit of those laws apart from obediently following the
letter, cannot help feeling how much has been done in this
direction, and how much this country owes to Kingsley
for stimulating others to take the work in hand. His
chief share consisted in removing prejudices against
sanitary measures by authority, and with others helping to educate public opinion to the extent of making
such Acts of Parliament more acceptable, and by them
to exercise that widely accelerative influence for the
betterment of local sanitary government, which requires more propelling power and moral momentum
to make it work effectually even in the present day.[1]

But apart from "State Hygiene," much is done now by
independent associations, such as the Ladies' Sanitary
Association founded in 1856, Canon Kingsley being one
of its earliest and most devoted friends, and where his

[1] It is only since the passing of the Local Government Act of
1888 that an "easy way has been opened for rural sanitary
administration."—*Sanitary Institutions*, by Sir John Simon, p.
420; cf. *Public Health Reports*, by the same, vol. ii. p. 364, *seq.*

memory is still cherished, as we are told—and we can well believe it—by its present able and active secretary. From its report for the year 1888 we learn that knowledge is growing on the subject among all classes, and with it a determination " efficiently to mitigate suffering and disease," and that there is a growing feeling among thoughtful women in favour of sanitary reform, and we wish the committee success in its expressed intention to " broaden out the lines on which reverent womanly preventive work may turn." This is exactly what Charles Kingsley strove and laboured for throughout. From its report for 1891 we learn that 10,000 sanitary tracts were disseminated in the previous year, making a registered total, since 1857, of 1,676,609. The general work of the society is very succinctly stated in its report presented to the Seventh International Congress of Hygiene and Demography held in the past year. It consists of lectures to ladies on physiology, applied to health and education, sanitary lectures for the artisan classes, instruction in educational gymnastics, depôt work in poor localities, providing baths, pails, tubs, brooms, &c., to promote personal cleanliness. The society has also opened a college for the technical training of girls of a higher grade in " hygiene and household science," and to provide lectures on nursing of the sick. In such and similar work it is carrying out those principles of sanitary reform of which Kingsley was the advocate, and on the lines indicated by him.

The National Health Society, to which he refers in favourable terms in one of his scientific lectures, organizes lectures in drawing-rooms and elsewhere on domestic hygiene, and by means of "Homely Talks" at mothers' meetings and workmen's clubs, endeavours to spread a knowledge of home-nursing and the prevention of infectious diseases. It holds examinations, awards prizes and a medal to those who prove themselves proficients in these subjects, and lately has worked in conjunction with county councils, providing lectures on food and cookery and the laws of preserving or restoring health. It, too, has a lengthy list of tracts to boast of. The Sanitary Institute, with its Parkes Museum in Margaret Street, founded a year after Kingsley's death, is an institution promoting similar objects. It holds sessional meetings, provides for lectures for sanitary officers, examines those who aspire to such offices, holds an annual congress like that on hygiene and demography already referred to, has a valuable library, and publishes works on sanitary subjects.

As a result of these and other agencies at work, Sir Joseph Fayrer, speaking on "Preventive Disease" at this congress, presided over by H.R.H. the Prince of Wales, and attended by thousands of visitors showing an enthusiastic interest in its proceedings, could state that in reference to sanitary progress in the country, great improvements have gradually been made (among the people) in the mode of living; the houses are better constructed, the drainage and ventilation are now complete, the land is better cultivated, and the subsoil drained . . . . the death-rate is considerably reduced, and the expectancy of life enhanced.

Water is purer, food is more varied and nutritious, clothing is better adapted to climate, the noxious character of many occupations has been mitigated, and the mental, moral, and physical aspects of the people altogether improved.   Education is general, a better form of government prevails, and the social conditions are far in advance of what they have been.[1] " But," he proceeds to say, " preventible disease still kills yearly about 125,000," and, " it has been calculated that 78¼ millions of days of labour are lost annually, which means £7,750,000 per annum."

Lord Basing, who was enabled to pass through Parliament the Public Healths Act in 1875, could boast at the same congress that in consequence of the administration of public health laws which that Act codifies and consolidates, the death-rate during twenty years has been reduced by one-seventh.   Mr. John Hamer (hon. secretary of the Mansion House Council on the Dwellings of the Poor) recommended, in the Section of State Hygiene, that railway companies should be compelled to run cheap trains within a fixed zone round every city for labourers and artisans coming from the suburbs and adjacent country; that lodging-houses should be provided by the enterprise of municipal authorities; and that medical officers of health should be State servants, not subject to property owners or the local authority, &c., &c.

From what has been said by such high authorities on the achievements of sanitary reforms, it is not

[1] *Times*, Aug. 12th, 1891.

too much to expect the favourable consideration of
such desiderata, and the acceptance of such a suggestion as that of Dr. Seaton, in his opening address as
President of the British Medical Association last year—
namely, the appointment of county healths officers, who
would be independent of local influences and authorities.
What has been done in the past augurs well for future
possibilities, and even so cautious and competent a judge
of such matters as Sir John Simon arrives at a hopeful
conclusion after a careful historical survey of the past
history of sanitary reform, so that in pronouncing his
sursum corda, he adds: " My thankfulness is not more
for the great interpreters of nature than for the men
who in nearer and more distinctive senses have been
the organizers of help for their kind, and have made
human sympathy a power in politics."

Among such men Charles Kingsley deserves a distinguished place.

CHAPTER IX.

IN THE PROFESSOR'S CHAIR, QUEEN'S COLLEGE, LONDON,
  AND CAMBRIDGE—THE SOCIAL SYSTEM TREATED
  ACADEMICALLY.

THE professorial career of Kingsley was cut short at
Queen's College for Ladies, Harley Street, to which he
was appointed on May 13th, 1848, and which he reluctantly resigned through ill-health in the spring of
1849. At Cambridge, where he held the Professorship
of Modern History from 1860 to 1869, he never felt
quite at ease, for both his unexpected appointment
and his work during the tenure of his office, as
Professor of Modern History, were made subject to
sharp criticisms, both within and outside the University.
Kingsley was too sensitive to bear these persistent
attacks with even-minded indifference, and too sensible
of his own deficiencies to regard them as entirely
groundless. Nevertheless, in his capacity as a lecturer
to young people of both sexes he exercised a potent
influence in helping to form opinions on historical,
moral, and social questions in his hearers and pupils
which have borne fruit since. Both in the Ladies'
College and at Cambridge, though in the first he still

was in the stage of youthful effervescence, whereas in the latter he had passed into that of ripened manhood, he tried and succeeded in stimulating and directing the appointed studies with a constant view to the social wellbeing of the nation. It was but natural that at Queen's College he should dwell chiefly on woman's sphere in the social system, whilst at Cambridge he would draw attention to the social lessons taught by history. Happily, his inaugural lectures in both places are available in a published form, so as to enable us to form an opinion on his collegiate work in this respect, and in them we have the pith and marrow of his teaching, his views on the relation of culture to social duty. These lectures should, however, be read in conjunction with some of his historical and general lectures and essays on sanitary and social questions delivered at the Royal Institution in London, the Philosophical Institution at Edinburgh, and other localities, for in them too he speaks as it were *ex cathedrâ*. They throw light on each other, and when taken together show more adequately than taken separately the balance and equipoise of Kingsley's mind, which some are inclined to give him little credit for. Note, for example, his strictures on the individualizing power which led to social dissolution in Alexandria during the Ptolemaic era, contained in his lectures on Neo-Platonism, and compare this with his qualified praise on the great work of the French Revolution in claiming the rights of a "God-given individuality," declaring, as he puts it, as Christianity had done eighteen centuries before, that "man is not the puppet of institutions"; and compare this again with his statements on the evil effects of excessive individualism, on which we have dwelt already, as the abuse of this divine right of personal freedom and responsibility; and from this comparative view on one single subject we may see how complete was Kingsley's grasp, though each taken singly would expose him to the charge of one-sidedness.

The two inaugural addresses at Queen's College are full of happy remarks on health and education, on woman's mission as a helpmate to man in the salvation of body and soul. In the introduction to his lecture on English Composition, written about the same time, he shows his lady pupils that the way to work out their great destiny is to educate themselves, since "woman is by her sex an educator," employed in the training of children; and so he concludes his lecture by reminding them "that it is the primary idea of this College to vindicate women's right to an education in all points equal to that of men; the difference between them being determined not by any fancied inferiority of mind, but simply by the distinct offices and character of the sexes."

So, again, at the commencement of his introduction to the study of English Literature, which also formed part of his teaching as lecturer at Queen's College, he expresses a fervent hope "that if this Institution shall prove, as I pray God it may, a centre of female education worthy of the wants of the coming age, the method and practice of the College will be developing, as years bring

Q

experience, a wider eye-range, till we become truly able
to teach the English woman of the nineteenth century
to bear her part in an era which, as I believe, more
and more bids fair to eclipse, in faith and in art, in
science and in polity, any and every period of glory
which Christendom has yet beheld."

And since knowledge puffeth up and charity edifieth,
he reminds his female audience that it is woman's
vocation to become " the priestess of Charity," that it
should be " one of the highest aims of woman to preach
charity, love, and brotherhood ; but in this nineteenth
century, hunting everywhere for law and organization,
refusing loyalty to anything which cannot range itself
under its theories, she will never get a hearing till her
knowledge of the past becomes more organized and
methodic."   Thus he concludes, in a fine peroration
which deserves to be transcribed in full, since it gives
an eminently sane and forceful view of woman's destiny,
fairly comparing with the best that has been written on
this subject, even by the greatest master of style—we
refer to the author of *Sesame and Lilies* and *Ethics of the
Dust.* Speaking of the purpose of the College, he says—

" Our teaching must be no sexless, heartless abstraction.
We must try to make all which we tell them bear on the
great purpose of unfolding to woman her one calling in all
ages—her especial calling in this one. We must incite them
to realize the chivalrous belief of our old forefathers amongst
their Saxon forests, that something divine dwelt in the
counsels of woman ; but, on the other hand, we must continually remind them that they will attain that divine
instinct, not by renouncing their sex, but by fulfilling it ;

by becoming true women, and not bad imitations of men ; by educating their heads for the sake of their hearts, not their hearts for the sake of their heads ; by claiming woman's divine vocation as the priestess of purity, of beauty, and of love ; by educating themselves to become, with God's blessing, worthy wives and mothers of *a mighty nation of workers*, in an age when the voice of the ever-working God is proclaiming through the thunder of falling dynasties and crumbling idols : ' He that will not work, neither shall he eat.' "

When Kingsley was compelled to give up his lectureship at the College, he writes to his successor in office, " Don't be afraid of talking about marriage. We must be real and daring at Queen's College, or nowhere ; " which was evidently meant as a hint, which at this time he thought fit to drop on all occasions, that " marriage is an honourable estate," not only as against the old and modern ascetics, as he does in the *Saint's Tragedy*, but also as against the fanatics of female education and idol-worshippers of art and culture, to declare once and for all, as Ruskin did, that education does not mean learned prudery or pharisaic pride in mental superiority, but is to be " enterprized," like marriage, not for the purposes of individual self-exaltation, but as a means of going on to perfection in the family or social unit, as the first step in the work of perfecting society as a whole. " The question of the better or worse education of women," he says in his lecture on " Thrift," delivered at Winchester in 1869, " is one far too important for vague sentiment, wild aspirations, or Utopian dreams." And further on, speaking of the effects of education on female character and habits, he says to the parents of women—

" If any parents wish their daughter to succumb at least to some quackery or superstition, whether calling itself scientific or religious—and there are many of both just now —they cannot more certainly effect their purpose than by allowing her to grow up ignorant, frivolous, luxurious, or vain ; with her emotions excited, but not satisfied, by the reading of foolish and even immoral novels . . . the immortal spirit, finding no healthy satisfaction for its highest aspiration, is but too likely to betake itself to an unhealthy and exciting superstition. Ashamed of its own long self-indulgence, it is but too likely to flee from itself into a morbid asceticism . . . never having been taught to guide and teach itself, it is but too likely to deliver itself to the guidance and teaching of those who, whether they be quacks or fanatics, look on uneducated women as their natural prey."

So, too, speaking on *technical education,* which has made of late such important strides in the direction indicated by Charles Kingsley, he expresses an intention of " restoring woman to her natural share in that *sacred office of healer,* which she held in the Middle Ages, and from which she was thrust out during the sixteenth century."

In the inaugural address to the study of English literature, he had spoken of History as a subject "most adapted to the mind of woman," because of the personal interest attaching to the men and women of whom history treats ; "the living human souls of English men and English women," and the interest in mankind, simply as mankind, which historical studies must have for woman, " with her blessed faculty of sympathy, that pure and tender heart of flesh, which teaches her always to find her highest interest in mankind, to see the Divine most completely in the human . . . to see, and truly, in the most common tale of village love and sorrow, a mystery deeper and more Divine than lies in all the theories of politicians, or the fixed ideas of the sage."

So, too, when appointed to the chair of Modern History in Cambridge, he still adhered to this method of directing the historical studies in his pupils. History was but his text, his chief aim was that of the teacher and preacher, and as an eloquent interpreter of the purposes of history before an audience of young men, to whom history is but too often a mere succession of events to be learnt by heart, and to be ready for periodical examinations, he achieved what he wished to achieve.[1] Accordingly, we find him saying in his inaugural lecture on " the Limits of Exact Science as applied to History," which appears as an appendix in the later edition of the *Roman and the Teuton*, that, as he is the greatest statesman who makes history because he understands men, so he is the true student of history who studies it because of, and only because of, the human interest in it.

[1] See F. Max Müller, Preface to *The Roman and the Teuton*, a series of lectures delivered before the University of Cambridge by Charles Kingsley, p. xii. This really is an apology on the part of the Oxford Professor, of his friend, bearing reference to the attacks of professed historians on Kingsley's want of accuracy and method.

" Names, dates, genealogies, geographical details, cos-
tumes, fashions, manners, crabbed scraps of old law, which
you used, perhaps, to read up and forget again, because
they were not rooted, but stuck into your brain as pins are
into a pincushion, to fall out at the first shake—all these
you will remember, *because they will arrange and centralize
themselves around the central human figure.* . . .

" Without doubt history obeys, and always has obeyed
in the long run, certain laws. But those laws assert themselves, and are to be discovered not in things, but in
persons . . . . though the rapid progress of Science is
tempting us to look at human beings rather as things than
as persons."

Thus, he would wish them to take the Roman's motto
for their own : *Homo sum, nil humani a me alienum
puto.*

It is interesting to follow Kingsley, who was both a
scientific and a literary man, in tracing the connection
between physical and moral or historical science, in
showing under what limitations history may be admitted
into what he calls elsewhere the " Choir of Sister
Sciences." In drawing the line of demarcation between the laws which govern natural phenomena and
human actions, he picks out an example in point which
is specially interesting in relation to the subject of this
volume, and to the economic controversies connected
with it. He speaks of the error of the early or *laissez-
faire* school of political economy.

" It was too much inclined to say to men, ' You are the
puppets of certain natural laws ' . . . no less certainly was
the same blame to be attached to the French Socialist
school . . . namely, that man was the creation of circum-

stances ; and denied him just as much as its antagonist the possession of free will, or at least the right to use free will on a large scale. . . . Both of them erred, surely, in ignoring that self-arbitrating power of man, by which he can, for good or for evil, rebel against and conquer circumstance."

He objects to the interpretation, therefore, of "moral phenomena by physical, or at least economic laws"; as a believer in the "self-determining power of the Individual," he holds that the inventive reason of man has been in all ages interfering with anything like an inevitable sequence or orderly progress of humanity.

His opinion as applied to this particular case is now accepted by nearly all the modern representatives of political economy and scientific socialism. Whether his argument applied universally, as against the opposite school of thinkers, will hold good, is another question. The preponderating influence of genius, and incalculable aberrations of the unreasoning multitude, as well as the unforeseen disturbances in the regular course of human action caused by monsters of virtue or of vice, make undoubtedly against the "regular sequence in human progress." There are things, as he shows with great force, which make it difficult to calculate beforehand the "effect of inevitable laws on human conduct"; there is, as he quotes from Goethe, in human nature a demoniac element defying all law and all induction.

Still it is questionable whether he gives here a complete reply to such arguments as those advanced by the late Professor Clifford, in some well-known Essays, or those underlying the philosophy of George Eliot's

novels on the close correspondence of the physical and
moral laws of our being. We take it that Kingsley
did not quite understand the terms of the controversy.
All that scientific interpreters of human action mean
is the existence of necessary laws of conduct, as sure
and unfailing as those which prevail in the physical
world ; and even Locke, in his work on the Human Understanding, gives a hint of the possibility of knowing at
some future date those moral laws of cause and effect
which would enable us beforehand to calculate events
in future history, though with our present limited
knowledge these do defy " exact computation."   But
Kingsley was right in pointing out the danger of
identifying physical and moral laws, apart from tracing
analogies between them, as tending to weaken the force
of the latter, since a materialistic conception of the laws
which govern human conduct acts as a moral solvent, and
must of necessity retard man's spiritual development.
Also in taking up the spiritual, as distinguished from the
mechanical view of social progress, he comes to a right
conclusion, though by a circuitous route of reasoning :
" If there be an order, or progress, it must be moral ;
fit for the guidance of moral beings ; limited by the
obedience which those moral beings pay to what they
know."   To this his opponents could not take exception.   But when he says, " man can break the laws
of his own being, whether physical, intellectual, or
moral," and on it founds his argument against *necessary*
laws, they would retort, and with a fair show of reason,
" Yes, and get broken on the wheels of natural necessity,

which ever revolve in the same round of cause and effect, whether you call it natural or supernatural law."

Both the subject and intention of this inaugural lecture, and the academical career of which it formed the commencement, suggest a comparison with one whose character and personal history were singularly like that of Charles Kingsley; we speak of Frederick Ozanam, sometime Professor of the Sorbonne, who, though a layman, made it the chief object of his life to defend Christianity against Scepticism, and to vindicate in the Professor's chair the spiritual as against the materialistic view of history. He too, like Kingsley, tried hard to impress the religious world with a sense of the importance of the social question, and its solution from the Christian standpoint. In his devotion to science, and the unrivalled power he possessed in attracting the young; in his belief in the sacred mission of art, as well as in the intensity of his own faith, and the corresponding power of raising it in others, he was the counterpart of Charles' Kingsley. Both were firm believers in the power of Christianity to effect a social palingenesis. They were contemporaries, Ozanam being Kingsley's senior by about six years. Both men also resembled each other in this, that they had their moments of weariness and *découragement*, which seems to be a peculiar trait of highly sensitive natures.

Ozanam, like Kingsley, became at an early age the recognized mouthpiece of the Christian party, and by his impassioned and sympathetic eloquence won brilliant triumphs in debate. Like the young law-students who

followed the lead of Maurice, a band of young French-
men with similar aims and aspirations gathered round
M. Bailly, and followed his advice to become the medium
of moral assistance and administration of physical
comforts to the poor of given localities; and out of
this sprang the powerful Society of St. Vincent de
Paul. Each member had a poor family to look
after; they met, like the band of Christian Socialists in
the house of Maurice, every week to report their experiences, discuss the wants of their *protégés*, and the
means of relieving them.[1]   Moreover, the relation of
Ozanam to the Socialists of France was not unlike that
of Kingsley towards the wilder sort of Chartists. "Free-
masonry," says Ozanam, and he speaks here as a devout
Catholic in the south of Europe, "and Socialism trade
upon the misery and the angry passions of these suffering multitudes, and God alone knows what the future has
in store for us if Catholic charity does not interfere in
time to arrest the servile war that is at our gates."
"Here are now (in 1840) 2000 young men enrolled in
this peaceful crusade of charity . . . giving everywhere
the password, *reconciliation and love.*"

It was the aim of both to "rehabilitate Christianity"
as the poor man's religion and the working-man's
friend, and both dwell, therefore, in their University
lectures by way of preference—Ozanam in a more
comprehensive manner than Kingsley—on the relation

---

[1] See an interesting memoir of *Frederick Ozanam, his Life and
his Works*, by Kathleen O'Meara (Grace Ramsay), with a Preface
by Cardinal Manning, 1878, pp. 79 and *seq.*

of Christianity to paganism, and the regenerative influence of Christianity socially in the early centuries of our era; and this with its bearing on present social difficulties. It is in 1848 that Ozanam thus speaks on the eve of the "violent shock" which perturbed England as well as France, and we hear almost the voice of Kingsley in what he says—"It is a social question; do away with misery, Christianize the people, and you will make an end of revolutions." The *Ère Nouvelle* took in France the place of *Politics for the People* in England; it was founded by Ozanam, and there are in it passages from Ozanam's pen describing the haunts of the poorer working-people in Paris, which bear a striking resemblance to similar descriptions in *Alton Locke*.

Like Kingsley, Ozanam belonged to the broader school of religious thinkers and workers, who endeavour to attract by affection rather than to compel by authority. He bewailed the extreme Ultramontane tendencies of the school of De Maistre, represented in the *Univers*, which only alienated the people in presenting the Church and Christianity in their most repulsive aspects. The aim of his own school, that of Chateaubriand, Gerbet, and Lacordaire, was like that to which in this country Kingsley belonged: "to search out all the secret fibres of the human heart that can attach it to Christianity, awakening in it the love of the true, the good, and the beautiful, and then showing it in revealed faith the ideal of those three things to which every soul aspires. Its mission is to bring back those who have gone astray, and to increase the number of Christians."

In the same way Kingsley showed indirectly in his lectures on Neo-Platonism that the secret of its failure, and the success of Christianity as a popular philosophy for all, consisted in this, that "there was a truly practical human element here in Christian teaching, purely ethical and metaphysical, and *yet palpable to the simplest and the lowest*, which gave to it a regenerating force which the highest efforts of Neo-Platonism could never attain." And this because the latter "refused to acknowledge a common Divine nature with the degraded man." Hence the "Alexandrian impotence for any practical and social purposes."

When in London during the Exhibition in 1851, Ozanam remarks on the wide gulf he observes to exist here between rich and poor; and he says, referring to this strange display of the extremes of wealth and poverty—"It looks to me like a seal of reprobation on their riches that they do not serve to ameliorate the lot of humanity—the lot, that is, of the greater number—and that the most opulent city in the world is also that which treats its poor most harshly." There is no need after all that has been said in this volume to quote passages from Kingsley of a similar nature. Enough has been said in drawing this parallel, which has an interest of its own, but serves more especially to bring out more clearly by way of comparison and contrast the characteristic traits of Charles Kingsley.[1] But in

[1] We may be permitted to refer here to an article originally published in the *Contemporary Review*, and afterwards republished in the author's work on Christian Socialism, on "Lamennais and Kingsley, a comparison and a contrast."

connection with the subject immediately before us in this chapter, we cannot avoid showing how both men, and for the reasons given already, were attracted to the same historical period in the selection of a subject for their academical lectures, because it afforded an opportunity for showing, as we said, the power of Christianity as a socializing influence, and its power for raising a society which was " expiring of over-luxury and wealth," and " its own corrupt excesses." From this they deduced the theorem that the same Christianity can save, too, our modern society. Ozanam, who " lived in the Middle Ages," takes for his watchword *Passons aux Barbares!* by which he meant the Germanic hordes, who after overrunning the Roman Empire were converted to Christianity. So far he and Kingsley are wide apart. But when we are told by Ozanam's biographer that his idea was " that religion could constitute this cohesive element in the State, that the Church would create the bond of unity, which would enable society to govern itself," we see that he was not so far apart from Kingsley's standpoint as might be imagined from the nature of the case. And in that portion of the volume on *The Roman and the Teuton* in which Kingsley dwells on the civilizing and organizing and colonizing work of the mediæval Church and monastic institutions, he is no less eloquent than his French neighbour, and no less ready than he to draw a lesson from it, that as " in the Middle Ages the masses rose by religion," so now the only hope of raising them permanently is through the power of Christianity.

The want of accuracy, and other faults of style and treatment in these Cambridge lectures have been made much of—too much we think—by Kingsley's severe critics. We need not dwell on this unpleasant subject here. Admitting the facts with some of Kingsley's most devoted friends, accepting his own self-depreciating remarks on his shortcomings in historical scholarship, we cannot help thinking that he was hardly dealt with. To him may be applied what he says in one of his lectures on the *Ancien Régime* (1869)—"Better for his race, and better, I believe, in the sight of God, the confusions and mistakes of that one sincere brave man, than the second-hand, cowardly correctness of all the thousand."

The great lesson Kingsley tried to impress on his hearers in the crowded lecture-room at Cambridge was the same as that which Ozanam, placed in a similar position, and as unfairly criticized at times by opponents, tried to convey to his pupils at the Sorbonne, that the future welfare of society depends on a new outburst of the latent forces of Christ's religion.

We have been informed by some who attended the Cambridge lectures, that in them there was little of social teaching, but those who have told us so attended only a few of these lectures. Every one who has taught in lecture-rooms or class-rooms, unless he is addicted to the vicious and wooden system of slavishly adhering to his manuscript or notes, knows how casual remarks, incidental thoughts, the result of sudden inspiration, come to the lecturer's lips, and are given utterance to and find lodgment in the hearer's memory. Certain it is that Kingsley stirred up the interest of young men, and in some way did divert their minds to social questions of the hour, as in the case of one whose letter Mrs. Kingsley quotes in the Memoirs of her husband, as one out of many expressing the general regret of the undergraduates when Kingsley left Cambridge—

"Speaking from the experience of these ten years, there is no comparison between our state of thought now and that of 1860—chiefly if not entirely due to you. We are learning, I trust, to look very differently at our relations to our fellow-men, *at those social duties* which seldom appear important to young men in our position, until we come across a mind like yours to guide us."

He once told a Fellow of the college with whom he was pacing round the cloisters in Neville's Court in Trinity after dinner, that all along he had been disappointed with his Cambridge residence and professorial successes, and, adds our informant, to whom the words were addressed, when Kingsley had lost confidence in himself owing to so much adverse criticism, which he was too modest to call in question, he lost the power of inspiring it in others. This may well be, and probably for this reason he left the University without resentment indeed, for there was no guile in him, and he was incapable of malignity, but also, we fear, without happy reminiscences. His gallant struggle to introduce a more humane study of history in Cambridge was a comparative failure. But, as he says somewhere in his historical studies, " no struggle after a noble aim, however confused or fantastic, is ever in vain."

CHAPTER X.

SUMMARY OF KINGSLEY'S ACHIEVEMENTS, AND ESTIMATE OF HIS LIFE AND WORK.

WE have now followed Kingsley through the greater part of his life, carefully keeping within the limits of the task undertaken in this volume, and that is to present him simply in the light of the social and sanitary reformer. We have shown how he was the man needed for the times, equipped by nature and prepared by circumstances and training for his work, and how ably and faithfully from first to last he did it, and this in the face of numerous obstacles, and at times under a deep sense of discouraging disappointment. We have seen him as the country parson practically carrying out those principles of social beneficence and self-devoted service to others which are so eloquently set forth in the *Saint's Tragedy* and his two social novels. We have seen him given up later on to the work of sanitary reform, and last of all as the Cambridge Professor, still adhering in the main to those social theories with which his name was identified in early life. Little remains to be said by way of summarizing his achievements, nor is it an easy task to form a correct estimate of an influence so varied as that which Kingsley exercised over the men and women of his day, an influence which, though real and extensive, was scarcely tangible enough to enable us to calculate its exact value and significance. Moreover, as we have taken pains at the close of each chapter to show what has been done since his day in the direction marked out by him, it is not needful here to dwell on these effects of his pioneering work. But the indirect influences of such a man are much greater than those which are patent to the eye. For Kingsley had a remarkable power over others, and much that they did was the result of his promptings and the effect of his propelling power, the magic force of his personality communicated to those who were under its spell. And this should not be left out in estimating the effect of all he was, and said, and did. But we might as well try to calculate with mathematical precision the circumference of all the circles formed at the most distant shores of the ocean by the ripples produced in the throw of stones by one standing at the opposite shore, and standing, as in this case, at some considerable distance from us both in time and space. Perhaps the best summary of Kingsley's varied gifts and graces, and the use he made of them, is that given by Professor Max Müller in the preface to the lectures on the Roman and the Teuton to which we have drawn attention already.

" As one looked on that marble statue which only some weeks ago had so warmly pressed one's hand, his whole life flashed through one's thoughts. One remembered

R

the young curate and the *Saint's Tragedy*; the Chartist parson and *Alton Locke*; the happy poet and the sands of Dee; the brilliant novel-writer and *Hypatia* and *Westward Ho!* the Rector of Eversley and his village sermons; the beloved Professor at Cambridge, the busy Canon of Chester, the powerful preacher in Westminster Abbey. One thought of him by the Berkshire chalk-streams and on the Devonshire coast, watching the beauty and wisdom of Nature, reading her solemn lessons, chuckling too over her inimitable fun. One saw him in town alleys, preaching the gospel of godliness and cleanliness while smoking his pipe with soldiers and navvies. One heard him in drawing-rooms, listened to with patient silence, till one of his vigorous or quaint speeches bounded forth, never to be forgotten. How children delighted in him! How young wild men believed in him, and obeyed him too! How women were captivated by his chivalry, older men by his genuine humility and sympathy! All that was now passing away—was gone. But as one looked on him for the last time on earth, one felt that greater than the curate, the poet, the professor, the canon had been the man himself, with his warm heart, his honest purposes, his trust in his friends, his readiness to spend himself, his chivalry and humility, worthy of a better age. Of all this the world knew little, yet few men excited wider and stronger sympathies."

Perhaps among these, one of the last-mentioned, his chivalry, was the most noteworthy, and Kingsley's insistence on the truth that, contrary to the well-known dictum of Burke, the age of chivalry is not past. "Some say," he preached in the chapel of Windsor Castle, "that the age of chivalry is past, that the spirit of Romance is dead. The age of chivalry is never past so long as there is a wrong left unredressed on earth, or a man or woman left to say, 'I will redress that wrong, or spend my life in the attempt.' The age of chivalry is never past, so long as we have faith enough to say, 'God will help me to redress that wrong, or if not me, He will help those that come after me, for His eternal will is to overcome evil with good.'" And in his own life he proved, as his wife has told us in a passage of touching pathos, that the age of chivalry has not passed away for ever, for "Charles Kingsley fulfilled the ideal of 'a most true and perfect knight' to the one woman blest with that love in time and to eternity." On account of this trait mainly, we venture to think, in his charming personality, Kingsley, as a man, as a minister, and as a man of letters, was so eminently successful in his social and sanitary mission. His modest manliness proved an irresistible attraction to all classes, to men of varied views, attainments, prepossessions, and even prejudices, and women were won over to the cause he advocated with so much genuine tenderness and heart-felt sympathy. His thoroughness, a rare quality at all times, not least so in his own day, imparted to all he said and did a living force which told powerfully on others. We come across a curious illustration of this in a letter of George Eliot, in which she says to Sarah Hennell (Nov. 26th, 1862)—

"You will be interested to know that there is a new muster of scientific and philosophic men lately established, for the sake of bringing people who care to know and speak the truth as well as they can, into regular communication. . . . The plan is to meet and dine moderately and cheaply, and no one is to be admitted who is not ' thorough ' in the sense of being free from the suspicion of temporizing and professing opinions on official grounds. The plan was started at Cambridge. Mr. Huxley is president, and Charles Kingsley is vice. . . . Mr. Robert Chambers (who lives in London now) is very warm about the matter. Mr. Spencer, too, is a member." [1]

How many clergymen at that date could be admitted on such conditions to such a club ?—how many still in our own ?

As a minister, Kingsley's power of persuasiveness again chiefly lay in the earnestness of his tone, the spiritual force of a man who deeply felt all he said and more, where every syllable was felt to be the outcome of a highly-wrought and finely-moulded mind ; it was the human element in him which endeared him to all hearts, as it was the forcefulness of his character which retained the esteem of those he had won by his affection. For this reason he never felt quite at home as a preacher in a university church. Here he never could get near enough to his hearers. In his village church and in Westminster Abbey he felt at home, for in both he could identify himself with his audience. Everybody loved him in his own parish, and all who cared for his preaching in London came to the Abbey to hear

[1] *George Eliot's Life*, by J. W. Cross, vol. ii. pp. 342, 343.

him if they could. In both places his sensitive nature was upheld by the responsive feeling of the audience; he was *en rapport* with his hearers. He was somehow conscious of the absence of this receptiveness in Cambridge. And this produced awkwardness, inward hesitation, and a corresponding lack of force. So, too, since the effect of spiritual force is in a given ratio to the effort expended according to the laws of conservation of spiritual energy, his work done so faithfully became in those who knew how to appreciate it a stored-up energy for good, an energy the effects of which are still felt in our own day.

As a man of letters he was not so much a "master of sentences," if by this be meant correctness of style and calm stateliness of diction, as he was able to express what he had to say with a racy, vigorous, "nervous grasp of words," introducing colloquialisms, and even slang when it served his purpose. There are occasional bursts of eloquence full of sublimity and pathos, and these are to be found by the side of quaint humorisms and grotesque turns of thought and expression, which produce the sense of unevenness in his best writings, and more so in the writings connected with our subject, for here he wrote and spoke over-mastered by his own emotions, which are too strong for controlled utterance. "With Kingsley," says Max Müller, "his life and his work were one. All he wrote was meant for the day he wrote it. He did his best at the time and for the time." That is, he wrote not for posterity, and, unless we are mistaken, for this very reason the immediate effect of his words was so great, and gave such a powerful impact to enthusiasms in young spirits, who were fascinated by his simple grandeur and naturalness. In this way he stirred up high-minded men and women of h's own day, and did much through them for intellectual and moral culture. Yet even among the best of these there would be some who felt as did George Eliot when she says, referring to Kingsley in one of her letters (we quote from memory)—" If you love him as much as I do, and are riled as much as I am by his faults." But what are minor faults, which offend the fastidious taste of the literary epicure, compared with the real force which made one of the wisest and most refined scholars of that day to say of him that, as he " walked amongst ordinary men," his walk " was often as of a waker amongst drowsy sleepers, as a watchful sentinel in advance of the slumbering host " ? A man of this sort struggling for utterance in the imminence of danger could not stay to pick his words. He could cry aloud and spare not, without giving heed to the tuneful modulations of his voice, or the measured cadence of his sentences. Had he done so, the dreamers would not have been awakened, as others, indeed, there were ready to lull them by their lullabies into pleasant optimistic dreams.

⁊ If we are asked what was the sum and substance of Kingsley's social teaching, we are inclined to reply in the happy phrase of a lady correspondent, speaking of Socialism, " What a curious copy and at the same time reversal of Christianity Socialism is ! " It was the great

aim of Kingsley to show how far Socialism could, and
how far it could not, be reconciled with Christianity;
how far they go together, and how far they were utterly
at issue. Few in his day, and not too many religious
and irreligious people in our own, taking an interest in
this question, were as clear-sighted as he was, and as
plain-spoken in pointing out the true and the false,
the attainable and the impossible, in the vague social
aspirations of the time, and in drawing a marked
distinction between the right and the wrong way, each
promising to lead to the goal. One of the greatest
services he rendered to his age was this, that he made
plain-speaking on such subjects popular, and so inspired
more timid Churchmen to have the courage of their
opinions then, and since, and to speak out their minds
without fear or favour, when by dint of intellectual
hardihood they had tackled with the social problem
honestly. Such plainness of speech, vigorous in proportion to its colloquial simplicity, as in his tract on
betting and gambling, or in his story *Westward Ho!*
could gain the ear of those for whom it was intended
by reason of its healthy masculine tone, which strikes
the ear of the young as a familiar sound. And more
or less this is true of most of his writings ; hence their
popularity among young readers, and their lasting effect
for good in fostering in them what virtue they possess,
and guarding them from harm and vices such as they
were prone to by reason of their youth. The young
officer and the young squire could read or listen to
Kingsley, but lent a deaf ear to all the dull discourses

of clerical pedants and respectable nonentities, who never depart a hair-breadth from the conventional tone whether in logic or in language, because of their *borné* attachment to systematic artificiality. There are the " spasmodic jerks and joltings as the steam-engine fights its way, with many an impatient snort, to its destination," as a contemporary critic complains, speaking of Kingsley's style, but there is also what the young call "go" in him. Even in the lecture-room, says the same critic, the extravagance of thought and language breaks out, "as if the shooting-jacket were peeping out under the Professor's gown ; the exuberance of animal spirits which explodes in slang, his fearless championship of what he believes to be truth, are the characteristics of one who retains the freshness and elasticity of mind which others have left behind them." And for this very reason, we reply, he was such an eminent Mentor of youths.

Kingsley was not exactly the founder of a new school, but he helped in forming a new school of the Prophets, a new order of truth-seeking and truth-speaking young clerics, whose distinctive characteristic is clergy-*manliness*, who in directness, spontaneity, and earnest simplicity which avoids the sanctimonious tone, but looks to true sanctity as the aim of all Christian teaching and life, are more or less influenced by the example of what Sir Mount Stuart E. Grant Duff calls the *openairness* in the tone and teaching of Charles Kingsley. These gradually displace the popular parson of the last generation. But the merit does not consist

only in helping to reproduce those of his traits which
are thought worthy of imitation in others, but also, as
the critic quoted above puts it fairly enough—and
coming as it does from an impartial contemporary it
carries great weight—

"If we look deeper we see in him a man fearless in
asserting the truth, as he conceives it, for its own sake,
and at all hazards, without being the slave of party;
who in an age of fastidious luxury not merely writes and
talks about the poor, but shows that he indeed feels with
them and for them; who keeps a practical aim in view,
while many lose themselves in impracticable doubts and
purposeless questionings; and who, while the world at
large is more prone than ever to bow the knee to
intellectual ability, is not ashamed to pay the honour
which they deserve to obscure labourers in the cause of
duty, rather than those who stand above their fellows
in the pride of knowledge and refinement. He sends
men back from unprofitable attempts to grasp what is
beyond their reach, to see that religion is really, as our
catechism teaches, the mainspring of morality, and that
the creeds of the Church Catholic find their fittest
counterpart in all that is noblest in man. He reminds
us that men are most truly 'manly' when they are
'godly,' that true manliness and true holiness are one.
An influence like this is especially efficacious among
young men, whose moral sense revolts from pharisaical
denunciations of the world as unmixedly evil, and from
the narrow timidity which, as in the Donatists of old,
so now in certain quarters, merges Christianity in the

cry, 'Shall I be saved?' They welcome in him a thorough Englishman, not exempt indeed from the weakness of his nation; an Englishman in politics, averse alike to a centralizing Imperialism and to a Republicanism equally subversive of domestic life; an Englishman in his religious belief, with nothing of Italian sentiment, of German scepticism, or of Calvinistic austerity about him, and whose watchword is that of our English Prayer-book, 'Fear God, and love your neighbour.'" [1]

Such an influence as here described by an independent authority, cannot but be efficacious for good, as the writer here quoted loyally acknowledges, and the question to be asked in the last place is, How far was it lasting? what will it be in the immediate future? Kingsley was eminently a "prophet of the present." He could not say with Carlyle a few days before his death, "They call me a great man, but not one believes what I told them." It was not true of Carlyle, for they would not read his books if they utterly disbelieve their contents. For the same reason it may be answered that the continued popularity of Kingsley's books are in some measure a proof of their vitality as a teaching power in the present day. But once more to quote Professor Max Müller, so high an authority, who knew Kingsley so well and lived with him on terms of intimacy both as a relative and a friend, and

---

[1] *Faith and Philosophy: Essays on some tendencies of the day,* by the Rev. T. Gregory Smith, late Fellow of Brasenose College, Oxford.

to apply what he says of the University lectures to Kingsley's writings generally : " They will be valued chiefly for the thoughts which they contain, for the imagination and eloquence which they display, and *last, not least, for the sake of the man*—a man, it is true, of a warm heart rather than of a cold judgment, but a man whom for that very reason many admired, many loved, many will miss, almost every day of their lives."

It is because in the words of Kingsley we hear the true ring of the human voice, addressed in tenderness to human beings like himself in search of a higher Human Ideal, that those words will find an echo in all human hearts, all at least not utterly void—if such there be, which God forbid !—of such higher individual and social aspirations, which to realize, Kingsley spent the whole of his life, and into which he threw all the strength of his noble soul, and thus " he being dead, yet speaketh."

THE END.

Richard Clay & Sons, Limited, London & Bungay.

14 DAY USE
RETURN TO DESK FROM WHICH BORROWED
LOAN DEPT.

This book is due on the last date stamped below, or
on the date to which renewed.
Renewed books are subject to immediate recall.